100 DISSERTATION MISTAKES

– 100 –
DISSERTATION MISTAKES

A COLLECTION OF ERRORS, FALLACIES, MYTHS, AND MISPERCEPTIONS

JOHN GARGER

ISBN-10: 069294396X
ISBN-13: 978-0-692-94396-0
23 22 21 20   10 9 8 7 6 5 4 3 2

The Science Survival Academy
Binghamton, NY
www.ScienceSurvivalAcademy.com

To doctoral students everywhere who persevere and succeed

.

CONTENTS

PREFACE

The genesis for *100 Dissertation Mistakes: A Collection of Errors, Fallacies, Myths, and Misperceptions* came from the many years I spent as a dissertation, research, and writing coach. While coaching doctoral students through their dissertations, I noticed that the same errors and misperceptions kept popping up across universities, fields, topics, methods, and students. I began tracking the mistakes that students make during a dissertation, and quickly compiled about 300 of them. The first few months of coaching are usually spent orienting students to the scope of a dissertation, and I recognized that I could reduce time spent on general mistakes and move more quickly to a student's specific problems if I compiled the most common mistakes into a book that would cost far less and take much less time than one-on-one coaching. I reduced the 300 I had compiled to 100 by combining several into a single mistake and removing the most obscure ones. The result is this book.

After considering most of the books published on the topic of dissertations, I noticed that none focus on mistakes. Some of my colleagues were concerned with this book's focus on mistakes, and one reviewer felt that I should not expose the topic using such a negative perspective. However, I have always been a firm believer in the adage that wisdom comes from experience, and experience comes from having made mistakes. The problem with dissertations is that there is no way to experience them more than once. A dissertation is like nothing you have ever done, and like nothing you will ever do again. This makes it impossible to experience a dissertation, learn from it, and do better the next time, because there is no next time. The next best thing to experiencing a dissertation for yourself is to learn from the mistakes of others, and that is why I wrote this book.

Assumptions

I had to make a few assumptions about dissertations and the students who conduct them to ensure that this book's content targets the right readers. I assume that doctoral students are required to submit a proposal that takes the form of the first 3 chapters of the dissertation, or is in the less common form of a prospectus, which contains fewer details on the study. Many of the mistakes discussed in this book assume that a dissertation requires some type of data collection and analysis, which is reasonable since most dissertations are empirical. I assume that a dissertation committee comprises multiple members, including a chair who oversees the student's progress with the dissertation, and that both a proposal and the dissertation itself must be defended to the committee's satisfaction. In some parts of the world, a dissertation is associated with a doctoral program, and in others with a Master's program. I use the U.S. tradition of associating a dissertation with a doctorate. I make no assumptions about the universities that doctoral students attend (e.g., ivy league, public, private, online, etc.), and I do not consider the sciences that they study (e.g., physical, biological, social, psychological, etc.). Consequently, not all of the mistakes discussed in this book are relevant to every student. I had to walk a fine line between discussing mistakes vaguely to appeal to all students and discussing them in detail such that they apply to only a few. Example mistakes from current and former students close that gap, which is why I include them, rather than just discuss them. The examples shared by students came from personal communication and e-mails, which I paraphrased for two reasons. First, some were very lengthy and I needed to reduce them to fit in this book. Second, I edited the examples to guarantee anonymity among contributors, facilitate the flow of the text, and retain common language throughout. For example, some universities call the chair of a dissertation a supervisor, senior advisor, or lead committee member. In such cases, I changed the designation to *chair*, the most common title given to the role, for consistency.

Concluding Remarks

Dissertations are a lot like a child; they embarrass you, they make you beam with pride, they make you cry, and sometimes they make you wish you had gotten a dog instead. I find that students fear dissertations simply because they think they are supposed to; they play the role of the struggling and overworked student, forgetting to experience a dissertation based on what is really happening, not an exaggerated version of it manufactured in imagination. I say this not to trivialize the dissertation experience but to demonstrate that if you think you can't do it, you are right. The misunderstandings that surround dissertations extend even into popular culture, and so doctoral students often approach them based on myth and misperception, which they carry through the entire process. This book demystifies dissertations by espousing a pragmatic approach—one that focuses on mistakes so students can learn from the experiences of others. Most doctoral students have similar experiences, requiring the same dedication, efficacy, and skills to complete a dissertation. Perseverance is the best predictor of dissertation completion, and by avoiding the most common mistakes, a clearer path to success emerges.

— BINGHAMTON, NEW YORK
September 2017

Acknowledgements

This book would have been impossible were it not for the hundreds of students with whom I had as many conversations. Their enthusiastic willingness to not only contribute to this book, but also help fellow students by sharing their stories, is laudable. I am indebted to their candid generosity. I thank two anonymous reviewers whose criticisms, praise, and recommendations shaped the tone and exposition of this book. I regret not being able to recognize them overtly for their contributions.

1

Perfect Storm

Climbing Mount Everest. Receiving a prestigious acting award. Winning a gold medal in an international athletics competition. All of these represent the pinnacle within their scopes of accomplishment. Similarly, a doctorate is a terminal degree—the pinnacle of scholastic achievement. Once a doctoral degree is conferred on you, you can go no further with your formal education. It is no wonder then that students perceive that the dissertation—the final step before conferment—must be worthy of this pinnacle status; the dissertation must be perfect, or at least as close to perfection as a student can achieve. Nothing could be further from the truth.

This book is not the first to suggest that doctoral students misperceive that they need to achieve dissertation perfection before their studies fill a gap, add to a topic's conversation, or otherwise contribute to a body of literature; most discussions of dissertations warn students of this common misperception. However, many doctoral students continue to believe in the perfection fallacy, and some even complete their programs still believing in it. A dissertation serves multiple functions beyond contributing to a topic's literature, but perfection has never been the goal of any study. Creating knowledge through science is an imperfect process. Every study has its limitations, and nearly all of the sciences require contributors to be candid about those limitations, usually in the form of a limitations section that appears in published articles. That section is not just obligatory; it represents inevitable imperfections that accompany knowledge acquisition through research. Just as journal articles are imperfect, so are dissertations. Chasing perfection in them is both futile and an impediment to completion. In a sense, the dissertation is a means to an end, and attempting to create perfection only prolongs programs and makes it less likely that a student will graduate. Consider Sarah's experiences:

I struggled with the design of my study, not so much because it was particularly difficult to isolate the variables or because I was doing something no other researcher had done before, but because I got caught up in a never-ending mode of improvement to make the design as good as it could possibly be. Even after my proposal was approved, I still kept trying to perfect the methods, proposing to my dissertation committee new ways that the design could be improved, to a point at which my chair told me, "Enough is enough! Move on with the remainder of the study." I was lucky that my chair stopped me because I could see myself improving the study's design *ad infinitum* until I perfected my way right out of my doctoral degree.

Michael experienced something similar:

The hardest thing I had to do during my dissertation was abandon it (i.e., submit it for final approval) because I wanted the writing in it to be a perfect example of scholarly prose. I figure that I wasted about 6 months trying to perfect my dissertation's writing, reexamining and tweaking the text so much that it became difficult to read. Spending 6 months longer in my doctoral program than I needed to meant that I had to take on more debt to pay for the program, and I was 6 months later getting into the job market. I figure that I spent about $65,000 in real costs and forgone salaries improving the writing—an expensive but very important lesson. It was a waste of time and money, so my advice to doctoral students? Finish your dissertation, but at some point, stop trying to make it perfect; the costs are too high if you do.

Although it is tempting to succumb to the euphoria that surrounds research, the creation of knowledge and the steps taken to acquire it are imperfect. The best dissertation is a signed dissertation, not a perfect one. Of course, that adage is also damaging if taken to extreme; no one is telling doctoral students to consider that since the dissertation is not about creating perfection that it is acceptable to be careless with the research they conduct. The point is that self-determined standards of quality sometimes get in the way of progress with a dissertation, so be mindful of perfection as a roadblock to completion.

2
Opus Fallacy

As terminal degrees, doctoral degrees carry with them prestige and the belief that they represent something great, even if that greatness is esoterically complex and obscure. They signal the end of formal education in a field, and consequently, many students perceive that the dissertation similarly represents the apex of their entire educational experience. Some students I have spoken to liken a dissertation to a final trial—pass or fail—that mirrors all of their education, from elementary school through to their doctoral studies. It is unsurprising then that the dissertation comes to symbolize the student's life work, a testament or pillar of scholastic achievement.

The dissertation is not your life's work, and nor does it summarize or denote your entire educational experience. The dissertation is a study, with which you demonstrate your ability to function as an independent researcher, thinker, scholar, etc. It contributes knowledge to a scientific topic and serves as an agent of learning for the student. Getting caught up in thinking that the dissertation represents a student's life work, compressed into a single manuscript, creates unrealistic expectations that cannot be achieved. The most successful doctoral students when it comes to completing a dissertation know from the beginning that the dissertation is an exercise in contribution, learning, and demonstration. It is a practical exercise, regardless of the lofty motivations and procedures that surround it. The dissertation is usually a student's first attempt at research. Expecting that it must represent the peak of a student's accomplishments is unrealistic for anyone—including the university, chair, or student—to impose on such an inexperienced researcher. Kara's characterization captures this sentiment well:

I spent over a year developing a topic for my dissertation, and I took so long that most of the members of my committee began to question whether I would finish. They began to lose interest in me, and some doctoral students who were a year or more behind me started to catch up to me in terms of completion. I had fallen into the trap of thinking that I had to create greatness to be worthy of the doctoral degree I was pursuing. I thought that the dissertation represented who I was and would eventually come to be an accomplishment with which people would forever judge me. When I stopped trying to impress people (and myself) and concentrated on making a serious contribution to my field, I found that the pressure to create something great subsided and I progressed toward completion much quicker.

Anna's experiences were similar:

I hate to admit it, but the dissertation was a mystery to me when I started thinking about my topic. I made the typical mistakes that doctoral students make at this stage, but I never truly understood what a dissertation was about or what it was supposed to achieve. In essence, I thought the dissertation was about me. I saw the dissertation as an opportunity to launch my career, and I believed that a poor dissertation, even if I completed the program, was tantamount to a career with which I would struggle. On what I now consider to be a fateful day, one of my committee members saw how much I was struggling to create a great dissertation, and he told me that the best dissertation was a signed dissertation. He also told me that most professors are at least somewhat embarrassed by their dissertations once they have been conducting research for about a decade or so. I slowly began to understand that my career would be judged by what I did during its entire duration, not by a single document that I compiled at its beginning.

Dissertations are difficult to complete, but students make them more difficult when they attach false perceptions of what a dissertation represents to them and others. Beyond the perfection fallacy, the second most common self-imposed barrier to completing a dissertation that students create is the belief that it must be great—a culmination of all of their education. The dissertation represents the end of something (i.e., formal education), but it also represents the beginning of a career. Abandoning the former and focusing on the latter will help you forgive yourself for not creating a dissertation that represents your life's work.

3
Onward Ultracrepidarian

Someone who talks, judges, or gives advice on a topic with which he/she has no knowledge is an ultracrepidarian. Novices are unable to create new knowledge within a topic, so it is surprising that many students think they can conduct research and contribute to the conversation on a topic in the literature (i.e., create knowledge) without first becoming an expert on the topic. No expert, not even your chair, is knowledgeable about every facet of his/her field. In fact, the more experience a researcher gains in a field, the narrower his/her expertise becomes because most researchers do not keep pace with all areas of their fields.

Suppose you need a tool to complete a home project, and you visit a home improvement store to buy it. When you arrive at the store, you go to the tool department, pick out a tool, pay for it, and leave. You do not peruse other departments in the store because you need only a single tool, and those departments do not pertain to your immediate needs. Many students treat their topics of study similarly, but in this case, the store represents the literature. They consult the literature only when they need something, and often skip those parts that do not pertain to immediate needs. This type of cherry-picking is an efficient way to use the literature, but it leads to negative consequences, most of which are felt at a much later time. Maggie experienced such consequences during her dissertation:

> During the coursework portion of my doctoral program, my cohorts and I usually took three classes each semester, each of which required us to read about 30 journal articles per week, for a total of 90 articles each week. With our other obligations in the program (e.g., teaching, research assisting, etc.), we found it impossible to read all of the articles each week. A former student in the program suggested that the most important content in a journal article appears in the abstract, introduction, and discussion sections, so to save time, I should read only those sections.

It seemed too good to be true, and it was. When I arrived at the dissertation stage of my program, I found that my knowledge was lacking when it came to research design and methods because I had skipped those sections during coursework. I essentially had to self-teach myself those topics, and I know that my program took longer as a result.

Rosalina was an ultracrepidarian in another way:

While working on my dissertation's proposal, I identified a gap in the literature and developed an entire study around it. I cited several studies many times, and built my case for the dissertation using a very narrow sample of the literature. After my chair and committee approved my proposal, I came across a study that examined the exact topic my dissertation was covering, and the results were either in the opposite direction I predicted or non-significant. Researching the topic further, I found an entire stream of literature that contradicted my hypotheses. After discussing it with my chair, I had to restructure the proposal into a different study, which took about three months to complete. My mistake was ceasing the literature search once I had what I was looking for and could develop what I had found into a study. I should have widened my search to gain an understanding of the entire topic, not just the parts that met my needs at the time.

No one expects a student to be an expert on all topics in his/her field, but it is reasonable to expect expertise with the topic to which he/she is contributing. Before deciding on a gap in the literature to fill, ensure that it is a gap, and that it has not been filled by literature that you have not yet discovered. You need to be an expert on a topic to contribute to its conversation in the literature. Becoming an expert on a topic in your field is not something that can be accomplished in a few days or even weeks. Getting a taste of a topic is insufficient to become an expert on it; you need to consume the entire topic before you can contribute to it.

4
Divided Attention

Assuming we exclude certainty (i.e., 100% probability of occurrence) and impossibility (i.e., 0% probability of occurrence), statistics tell us that the probability of event A occurring is more likely than the probability of events A and B occurring simultaneously. This is true in all cases, regardless of what the events are. This relationship applies to real-world events, even when it comes to the probability of success with a dissertation. The probability of completing a dissertation while your attention is divided by other pursuits drops tremendously, and in ways you might be unaware of or cannot predict.

While coaching students through their dissertations, I always offer one piece of advice. No matter how long you think something will take to do—design the study, collect data, analyze data, etc.—multiply it by 3; if you think designing the study will take 3 weeks, figure it will take 9. Murphy's Law pops up more times during a dissertation than you can count, and not everyone involved with the study (e.g., chair, committee members, graduate school, etc.) will be available when you need them; such actors seemingly disappear just when you need them most (e.g., winter break, vacation, retirement, illness, etc.). Scheduling their limited time around your limited time can be impossible, and the person who needs to be flexible with time is you. Splitting time between your dissertation and some other major part of your life, especially work and changes to lifestyle (e.g., marriage, divorce, having a child, etc.), creates time demands that interfere with completion of a dissertation. Students have control over some of these, but no control over others. Therefore, it is vital to manage those over which you have control to maximize your chances of completing the dissertation, and ultimately the program. Barry ran into this problem during his dissertation:

I was pursuing my doctoral degree at the same time I was working full time. I thought I could devote all of my nights and weekends to the dissertation and avoid having to quit or reduce my work hours so I could have a steady income and avoid taking out loans to pay for the program. Unfortunately, the company I worked for started facing fierce competition and we all had to work overtime to compensate. I had to place my dissertation on hold for over 6 months. I didn't want my chair to know that I was working full time while working on the dissertation so I did the minimum to keep the program alive by submitting small updates to her that were weeks apart. I was able to finish the dissertation, but I wonder how much smoother it would have gone and better it would have been had I focused full time on it.

Antony's experiences were similar:

I took a teaching job at a nearby technical college just at the time that I started my dissertation. I soon found that the dissertation was taking too much of my time away from teaching. More than a few times, the dissertation and teaching conflicted, and I had to choose between the two. Since the dissertation could be worked on at any time (i.e., nights, weekends, holidays, etc.), teaching usually won. That proved disastrous since I was behind on my dissertation by about 4 months by the time the semester ended at the technical college. I learned the hard way that I could not divide my time between the dissertation and anything else. No career jumpstart was worth jeopardizing the dissertation and consequently finishing my doctoral program. I would advise doctoral students to carefully consider whether taking hours away from a dissertation is worth it.

Dissertations are not part-time endeavors; they require full attention to increase the probability of completing them. Dividing your time between the dissertation and anything else non-essential makes completion much less likely. I recommend that about 6 to 12 months before you start your dissertation that you begin clearing your schedule and consider what is truly essential that you cannot give it up, at least temporarily, so you can work full time on the dissertation. Since the dissertation is an unstructured task (i.e., there is no set time you must work on it), it often gives way to structured tasks, and they fill your time rapidly.

5
My Kingdom for a Horse

Even doctoral students who have some say in who becomes the chair of their dissertation are subject to practical limitations regarding who sits in that seat. Some professors are serving as chairs or committee members on other dissertations, and others are planning sabbaticals, disqualifying them as chair candidates. Even with these limitations, students usually have some input, either directly or indirectly, on who serves as chair. However, students commonly wait too long to consider their choice or are unaware that they have some say, resulting in a mismatch between student and chair regarding approach, work ethic, personality, dedication, goals, etc., making it less likely that the student will finish the dissertation.

Although most students perceive that a dissertation is a rigid undertaking that involves adherence to scientific principles, evocation of the highest ethical behaviors, and following rules of engagement, dissertations are much more social than they appear. The best situation a doctoral student can be in is to have a potential chair who is genuinely interested in serving in the role. Getting a professor to that point requires more than a one-time pitch of a proposal; it requires some socializing that involves getting to know one another professionally, especially regarding the student's career plans, and research and teaching interests. I am not talking about schmoozing; I am talking about the inability of people to get excited about working with someone else when the first time they talk about a project is the day it begins. This is a time when university procedures walk a line between the formal and informal, and being unprepared means that some dissertations get off to an inauspicious start. Robert's story exemplifies this experience:

9

I had no idea that I could choose the chair of my dissertation. I assumed that someone would be assigned to the role and we would begin working from there. I was surprised when my advisor asked me for a list of professors I would like to serve as my chair and on my committee. I had to search around my former professors for someone who was not currently serving as a chair for another student, was willing to serve as my chair or on my committee, and had the time to serve in those positions. Those three criteria were difficult to find in one candidate. I spent several weeks doing the legwork, and in the end, the person who served as my chair was the fifth choice on my list. Had I known I had a say in the matter, I would have started the search much sooner.

Steven's story demonstrates a direr situation:

The biggest mistake I made with my dissertation was also my first. I seemed to be the only doctoral student in my cohort who was unaware that we needed to choose our own chairs. How this fact escaped me is beyond my comprehension, but let my ignorance serve as a warning to other doctoral students. By the time I realized my mistake, most of the professors available to be a chair were already allocated to other students. The next one who would become available wouldn't be finished with his current student for another 4 months. My advisor was able to get that professor to be my chair and told me to just work on my dissertation proposal until the other students finished and the professor could turn his attention to me. I had no idea that the process worked that way. I just assumed that a chair would be assigned to me because I was "owed" one. I didn't know that a relationship had to be forged between chair and student that way.

Dissertations are constructed much more socially than intuition suggests. Students sometimes relate extreme cases in which they could not find a professor to be their chair and a professor had to be begrudgingly assigned to them. The lesson here is to start looking for a chair early, and be explicit about your interest in having your choice serve as your chair when the time is right. Waiting too long and assuming how the process works can cost a doctoral student dearly in terms of idle time and the probability of finishing the dissertation and program.

6
Birds of a Feather

Students who are aware that they have some control over who becomes their chair commonly choose a professor for the wrong reasons. The most common include similar research interests, clout regarding career advancement and networking, and affect due to admiration or friendship. The problem with these criteria is that they have nothing to do with whether a chair can see a student through a dissertation; they indicate nothing about the relationship that will develop between the student and chair. It is common for doctoral students to forge strong working relationships with their professors, some of which even evolve into friendships. However, when it comes to choosing a chair for a dissertation, an objective choice is best.

There is no such thing as dissertation chairing school, and most of the professors I have spoken to regarding their chairing experiences admit that they received little training on how to manage, lead, and oversee students during their dissertations. Academia assumes that once you hold a doctoral degree, you can operate skillfully in any position you hold in the ivory tower, including overseeing a doctoral student transition from student to independent researcher. The best choice you can make when selecting or requesting a chair is to find someone who will see you through the program, and that means being objective and truthful about the skills and personalities of the professors who are available to serve as your chair, regardless of your personal feelings about those professors. Many doctoral students perceive that their chairs are being negligent, though most of the time the chairs are simply giving the student room to demonstrate the transition to researcher. Still, at least some guidance is needed, and having a chair who recognizes and provides that need is more important than a match based on research interests, career advancement, and affect. Kathryn's experiences suggest this is true:

> When searching for someone to be the chair of my dissertation, I thought I found a good match in a professor who shared the same research interests that I had. In fact, she was the reason I became interested in my field. However, after I started working on my proposal, it became obvious that she had too many things on her plate to devote much time to me and my dissertation. It would take days, and occasionally weeks, to hear back from her over e-mail on even the simplest of issues and questions. Part of the problem is that she was very disorganized, and often had to be reminded of what we talked about during previous meetings. On more than one occasion, she critiqued the wrong version of what I had sent her, dragging the process out even further. Her personality and approach to research was so different from mine that I nearly didn't finish the program because of it. I should have considered her personality rather than her expertise when I chose her for my chair.

Chris experienced something similar:

> I chose my chair based on the relationship I developed with him during the coursework portion of my program. However, he was a very different chair in comparison to how he taught. His passion for teaching was well known among the graduate students, but he seemed to have little passion for research. I could never get a straight answer from him, and occasionally he seemed ambivalent about my progress with the dissertation, seemingly faking his way through the process. He seemed to be different people when it came to teaching versus chairing. I should not have assumed that his passion for teaching would translate into passion for everything he does.

If you have some say in who your chair will be, consider carefully the attributes you use to determine whether someone will be a good match for you as chair. Simply belonging to a category (e.g., passionate teacher, good publishing record, vast networking, etc.) does not mean that you will work well with that chair. The most important attributes have to do with whether a chair will see you through the program. This is a time when tough decisions must be made, and it is a time for a doctoral student to begin thinking like an independent researcher.

7
Here Is Your Map

Learning occurs similarly from kindergarten through doctoral coursework. A student is given pieces to a puzzle, and he/she is shown how the pieces assemble to create a picture. The pieces are then disassembled, and the student demonstrates that he/she can assemble the pieces into that same picture. The degree to which the student assembles the puzzle pieces into the predetermined picture determines scholastic performance. Most topics, including math, language, and even the arts, use this or similar pedagogies, but dissertations do not operate this way. Not only is the student not shown how the puzzle is assembled, he/she is not even given the pieces. The student must find his/her own pieces and assemble them into a new picture.

Leaders often initiate a structure, including rules, boundaries, obligations, and goals, so followers can succeed. Such initiation provides followers with a map so that they can navigate the terrain of a project or task. Pre-dissertation learning at all levels between an instructor and student operates similarly, and doctoral students are therefore surprised when their chairs provide little guidance on how to get started with a dissertation. Doctoral students commonly hesitate because they are waiting for a chair to produce puzzle pieces or maps so they can begin. Transition from student to researcher requires that students demonstrate independence, and so dissertations require that students find their own puzzle pieces to assemble and draw their own maps to the completion of their dissertations. Connie hesitated at the beginning of her dissertation:

> After passing my comprehensive examinations, I was excited but nervous about beginning my dissertation. My chair and I discussed what was required of me in the technical sense, but we did not discuss the specifics of how I would accomplish the tasks. I felt like a racehorse in the starting

gate who was waiting for the bell to ring and gate to swing open so I could start running, so I was concerned when some of my cohorts seemed to be progressing with their proposals and I was seemingly standing still. Had the bell rung and I missed it? Had my chair forgotten about me, or was she waiting for some free time to tell me what to do? After about a month, I mustered the courage to ask her what she wanted me to do. She was surprised that I had not started, and that I had nothing to show given that a little more than 30 days had passed since I "began" working on my dissertation proposal. I assumed that she would provide more guidance with the dissertation, and I learned the hard way that students must proceed alone on the dissertation journey.

Karen's experiences were similar:

My dissertation did not begin well because I misunderstood the chair's duties and function. I thought of a chair as a type of guide—someone who would accompany me on the dissertation journey and tell me when I was approaching a dangerous situation or following the wrong path. I don't know why I thought that, but I soon found out that I was wrong. The professors during my doctoral program were friendly, dedicated, and a joy to learn from. They made my topic come alive for me, and I looked forward to the one-on-one relationship I would have with one of them during the dissertation. I was relieved when I was assigned my first choice for chair of my dissertation. However, right from the beginning, my chair seemed more distant than usual, and she rarely answered my questions directly. This was hardly the guidance I thought I would get from her. I came to find out that I needed to proceed alone, and that the chair plays the role of judge rather than guide. I am glad that I discovered this sooner rather than later because I had begun to interpret her distance as disinterest in me and my research topic.

Were doctoral students guided heavily through their dissertations, they would not have the opportunity to demonstrate the independence that represents being a researcher. No profession that requires independence on the part of its practitioners would benefit from pedagogies that include holding students' hands. The dissertation must therefore be an independent journey so that it creates an independent researcher when the journey ends.

8
Where art Thou?

Dissertations are lengthy, time consuming, and complex, making it difficult for students to remain on schedule. Even more difficult is keeping track of how a student is progressing with a dissertation, especially since days, weeks, and sometimes even months pass between contact with a student regarding that progress. Professors are busy professionals, and it is easy for them to lose a student in the shuffle. The *out of sight, out of mind* aphorism applies commonly to the relationship between chair and student, and consequently, students should not find it surprising that chairs often lose sight of a dissertation's progress.

Exacerbating this is the fact that students are apprehensive about looking foolish in front of a chair. Professors experience a lot of pressure, both self-induced and from the environment, to project an air of intelligence, capability, and accomplishment, and if you are like most students, you have already begun to experience those same pressures. Students often avoid a chair when they perceive that they have not made sufficient progress with a dissertation to warrant an update to the chair. Consequently, students often disappear from their chairs for long periods, making it difficult for chairs to remember what occurred during the last few meetings or updates. Time is the biggest enemy here. Don't assume that your chair knows where you are with the progress of your dissertation, and don't be surprised if your chair misperceives your progress, either less or more than its true state, if contact with your chair is fleeting and infrequent. Denise shared this story with me:

> I was experiencing writer's block on a section of my dissertation, and it had been several weeks since I last spoke with my chair as a result. When he finally contacted me, asking for an update, I mentioned the trouble I was having. I was stunned when he told me that he thought I was done with that section and that I should have been done with a subsequent

section by now. I never felt such pressure to progress with the dissertation, and I was careful to inform my chair of my progress, or lack of it, from then on.

Joseph's story is much more intense:

I wanted to finish my doctoral program by the end of the year, which means I needed to have defended my dissertation by October to make the thesis office's and graduate school's deadlines for graduation in December. I told this to my chair in late July, and I knew that I needed to hurry to finish the dissertation by August to allow time for review by the committee and scheduling of my defense. Sometime in late August, it became apparent to me that I would not make graduation in December, so I slowed the progress of my dissertation and resigned myself to a May graduation. Unfortunately, I forgot to tell my chair about my progress, and thinking I was still on track, he scheduled my defense without me knowing about it until early September. I assumed that he would wait to hear from me before scheduling the defense. Since the defense could not be canceled, I worked about 80 hours per week through the rest of September and into October to deliver the dissertation. I got it done, but I realize now that I should not have assumed that my chair knew where I was with the dissertation, or of the decisions I had made. I blame myself, and I would inform my chair of my progress more often if I could do it over again.

Dissertation chairs are human beings; they are subject to the same personal biases as anyone else, especially since they are busy and need to track many projects simultaneously. It might dismay you to hear this, but you are just one part of your chair's life, and you are not likely the most important part. Your chair has a career to consider, and many other students to teach. It is up to you to inform your chair of your progress, or lack of it, if you want your chair to have a clear picture of where you are with your dissertation. Otherwise, the consequences can be costly to you.

9
Hero Worship

Management and leadership theories suggest that subordinates often admire superiors for their charisma, and use a superior as a model to shape their own behaviors, accomplishments, principles, and even mannerisms. Consequently, it is common for doctoral students to wish to be the researchers that their chairs are, which is a healthy practice because it provides a baseline and set of standards to follow. However, sometimes admiration goes too far, and subordinates fail to see the flaws in their heroes, creating an unrealistic standard to achieve.

Doctoral programs and dissertations are difficult to complete. If they weren't, far more people would pursue doctoral degrees. Consequently, doctoral students often look for shortcuts and ways to reduce the time and effort spent on a portion of the dissertation, and nothing seems more gratifying than when a chair gives a student a clear directive or advice. Unfortunately, that can work against the student when the directive or advice is flawed. Your chair is fallible in research, and not everything that chairs tell students is correct. Kelly shared a fascinating story with me on this topic:

> I will admit right away that I was (and still am) terrible with statistics, so it is a wonder that I chose a quantitative design for my dissertation. I was struggling with the size that my sample should be, and I asked my chair for advice. He offered, "Oh, I'd say about 200 to 250 should suffice." I was glad to get a straight answer from him, so I planned to achieve that sample size for my study. After data were collected and it was impossible to increase my sample size by drawing from the same population, I learned about statistical power, which is a function of sample and effect sizes. One of my committee members, an expert in statistics, required me to calculate the power of my analyses. Since the literature suggested I would achieve only small effect sizes, I needed a sample size of at least 800 to

achieve statistical power of 0.8, which is the threshold the literature suggests. I fell far short of that threshold, but luckily my committee allowed me to continue since I had sufficiently demonstrated that I could conduct research beyond this one mistake. When it came time to publish the findings from my dissertation in a journal, the statistical power issue prevented me from doing so. I appreciated everything my chair had done for me, but his quick answer—and my blind acceptance of it—cost me quite a bit.

Adam experienced a similar situation:

 After the defense of my dissertation, I had just two weeks to submit my dissertation to the graduate office for approval of the manuscript's format. The standard I was using requires a journal article's volume and issue numbers to appear in the references. I admit that even today the idea of dealing with the tedium of formatting references makes me cringe, and with over 300 references, I had a lot of work ahead of me. I mentioned this casually to my chair, and he told me that the graduate school did not require issue numbers, which cut my work in half since I now needed to include only volume numbers. When I submitted my dissertation to the graduate school, I was told that I needed to include the issue numbers before the dissertation could be approved. I had no choice but to spend 24 sleepless hours looking up and adding the issue numbers to the references. I wish I had found out for myself what I needed to do instead of relying on my chair's advice.

When people build up a hero to standards that are impossible to live up to, they are disappointed nearly every time. Making a hero out of a dissertation chair is easy since professors are able to hide their mistakes easily, further helping them project the image of perfection and competency that they feel compelled to project. Your chair is capable of mistakes and being misinformed as much as anybody is. When faced with a problem that could cost you, be careful that your fatigue and need to remove something from your plate do not entice you to proceed without verifying for yourself what you need to do.

10
Perpetual Motion

Everything you need to do to finish your dissertation will take longer to complete than you will expect it to. Consequently, most doctoral students use nights, weekends, and holidays just to keep up with the amount of work that goes into a dissertation. Unfortunately, this leads to poor eating habits, little exercise, and sleep deprivation, all of which make the dissertation that much more difficult to complete. The human body requires rest, exercise, and a proper diet to function optimally, so in a way, spending less time on a dissertation gets it done quicker and better.

The most successful people worldwide are highly dedicated to their work, but they know that health and happiness are essential to achieve success with that work. They know that the harder they work at something, the less time they have to work on themselves, which degrades their efficiency and makes finding more time to work necessary. This can create a vicious cycle during which inefficiency breeds more inefficiency. Taking the time to enjoy aspects of life other than your dissertation, such as exercise, time spent with friends and family, and even time pursuing a hobby, increases your efficiency and motivation to work on and complete your dissertation. This is a case of *the harder you work, the less you get done.* Jennifer discusses this topic:

> While working on my dissertation, it seemed like there was never enough time to get everything done. To make up for what I thought was insufficient time, I started eating a lot of fast food, got nearly no exercise, and began alienating myself from my family and friends. I often had symptoms associated with the flu, and my body ached while I sat hunched over my computer trying to work on my dissertation. Eventually, I had to take leave from my program for a few months to deal with my health. I learned that concentrating nonstop on my dissertation was causing me to develop depression, which only distanced me from finishing my dissertation. When I resumed work on the dissertation, I limited myself to 40 hours,

and I started a regular program of exercise, healthy diet, and time spent away from the dissertation. I completed the dissertation, and I was much happier while doing it.

Victor had this to say:

While working on a dissertation, everything else seems expendable, especially your diet and sleep. You can easily get caught into a trap of using every waking moment to work on the dissertation, ignoring even warning signs that you are working too hard. Exercise and a good diet are the two most important components to working well, even if it means working less on the dissertation than you technically could were you to avoid them. During my dissertation, I developed eye strain and headaches from staring at a computer screen for over 60 hours each week. They were minor annoyances, but others might develop more serious illnesses if they don't take the time to step away from the dissertation once in a while. When you do, you start with a fresh perspective when you resume working on it, which only helps you complete it more quickly. My advice to doctoral students who are working on their dissertations is to track your time spent on the dissertation and determine the hour at which your abilities drop below when it is worth continuing. Take a walk, take a day off, drink lots of water, and get plenty of exercise and sleep. Nothing will get your dissertation over quicker than making those things a permanent part of your routine.

You are not a machine; your body and mind need nourishment and rest to function well. Working harder at a task can lead to less work getting done, not more, when taken to extreme, and can even derail a dissertation when illness and fatigue take over. Take advice from some of the most successful people in the world and make some time for yourself. Not every problem you encounter during your dissertation must be solved as quickly as possible, even though the urgency experienced by doctoral students during a dissertation suggests otherwise. A dissertation is a learning experience. Do not conquer it. Enjoy it.

11
Key Worker

In business, a *key worker* is someone who is so essential to the operation of a company that his/her absence due to illness or another impediment to working, such as legal trouble or incarceration, is tantamount to the business ceasing to operate. Sole proprietors and headlining talents are examples of key workers. As the only person who can complete your dissertation, you are your dissertation's key worker, and therefore keeping you on task is essential to the dissertation moving forward and getting completed. However, some tasks during a long-term project can be completed by others, and pushing those tasks to them frees up a key worker's time to concentrate on more important aspects of the project.

A dissertation inevitably takes a lot of time to complete, and it often requires students to work on mundane, low-value-added tasks that take time away from bigger, more important aspects of the dissertation. Prioritizing is essential to any project that takes up a large portion of your time, including a dissertation, meaning that you need to categorize tasks into those that must be completed by you and those that can be completed by others. As the key worker of your dissertation, you need to determine what tasks belong on each side of the table so you can decide which to concentrate on and which to avoid. Unless the rules set forth by your university or chair forbid you from doing so, consider getting help with the mundane aspects of the dissertation, including obtaining articles, verifying the formatting of citations and references, etc. Key workers in an organization don't clean bathrooms, stand in line at a photocopier, or vacuum the floors. Similarly, you should be concentrating as much as possible on the design of your study, how you will collect data, how you will analyze the data once you have them, etc., not on mundane, low-value-added aspects of the dissertation. George's story reflects this advice:

My dissertation included many tables, figures, and equations, and I found myself spending too much time creating these important but time-consuming parts of the document. One of my cohorts recommended that I hire a graduate student to help with these tasks, but I was leery about spending money on something I could do myself. I eventually hired the graduate student, and I found that the time I got back by not having to do those tasks myself was more than worth it. It was like I was buying time back, and time is something a doctoral student never has enough of. I did the math and I figured that since I finished the dissertation nearly a semester ahead of schedule, I saved thousands on tuition and loan interest, and I was in the market about 4 months earlier than I would have otherwise been. It was money well spent because it was an investment in myself.

Nancy experienced something similar:

I know that I am a good writer, but editing one's own text is a bad idea because writers tend to read what they think they wrote rather than what they really wrote. I decided to hire a copyeditor to edit my dissertation one chapter at a time as I completed them. The cost was moderate, but once I got the copy-edited text back from the editor, I knew I was done. I simply compiled the chapters and submitted the dissertation for approval. This left me more time to work on the content of the dissertation and not the details I could pay someone else to do. I am a firm believer in *work smarter, not harder*, and sometimes that means pushing some work to someone else so you can work on what really matters.

Being a good key worker means discerning what matters (i.e., the things only you can work on) from what matters but can be done by anyone (i.e., outsourcing) so you can concentrate on the big picture. Seeing yourself as the key worker in your dissertation helps you see that big picture. If cost is a concern, consider that more time spent in a program means a far greater cost than hiring someone temporarily who can help you finish it sooner. There is a tradeoff here, but one that should be considered in a business-like manner.

12

Working Vacation

A dissertation is a long process of theorizing, analyzing, writing, and personal transformation that inevitably makes a student loathe and avoid it. Some students even begin to perceive that not graduating is more appealing than finishing the dissertation. Countless chairs have told me on many occasions that perseverance is the strongest predictor of whether a student finishes a dissertation, not knowledge or innate ability, and working on a dissertation without taking long breaks is the best way to prevent negative feelings about a dissertation from festering into despair.

Although you cannot work on a dissertation constantly, due to both bodily and cognitive limitations, and demands from other aspects of your life, taking a long break from a dissertation is usually a sign that a student has encountered a barrier, either real or imagined. They confuse the feelings they have about the barrier for the barrier itself, and believe that avoidance will make the barrier disappear as soon as the negative feelings subside. However, avoidance only makes the barrier more difficult to traverse because worry about not being able to overcome a barrier creates stress that in turn lowers a student's ability to overcome it. Avoidance is a slippery slope. Students who fall prey to the slippery slope of avoidance believe that a break, which commonly turns into a long one, will recharge their ability to overcome an obstacle, but they usually just end up burying themselves in menial tasks that are external to the dissertation to justify the avoidance. The result is an unfinished dissertation, and an uncompleted program. Roxanne almost succumbed to the slippery slope of avoidance:

> The design I used during my dissertation was complex, and during analysis of the data, some hypotheses were unsupported, which made comparisons across results impossible. Such comparisons represented the purpose of the study, so I thought the dissertation was over and I would have

to either collect new data or develop an entirely new proposal. I avoided the issue by not working on the dissertation for nearly 5 months. During that time, I got involved in several activities that distracted me from the problem. Eventually, my chair asked me about the progress I was making with the dissertation, and I was forced to come clean. To make a long story short, the data and analyses were salvageable because my chair and I worked on refocusing the dissertation to remove having to compare results to achieve the purpose of the study. I had nearly quit the program because I could not see that third possibility.

Stan experienced something similar:

Early during my dissertation, I could not get beyond the pre-proposal stage because I could not justify my hypotheses with a theory that my chair approved of. I began to doubt my ability to finish the dissertation because I thought I was experiencing a Catch-22—I could not figure out a solution to my problem alone, and I was not allowed to ask for outside help with the problem. It didn't take long for me to immerse myself for two months in projects that made me feel in control. However, thoughts about my dissertation dilemma loomed over me like a cloud. One day I got the courage to ask one of my committee members for help, and within two weeks we had largely solved my problem and I was back on track. My assumptions regarding what I was and was not allowed to do nearly cost me my doctoral degree, and I realize now that I should have tested those assumptions earlier.

Avoidance is common when facing a seemingly insurmountable obstacle, especially when working independently and no one is monitoring the progress regularly. I advise students to take breaks only when milestones are reached. The 1-day/3-day principle is a good heuristic to follow. Take one day off when you reach a minor milestone (e.g., completion of a major section of a chapter, finishing a major portion of data collection, etc.), but take 3 days off when you reach major milestones (e.g., completion of a chapter, completing data analysis, etc.). If you find yourself taking more time than that, look objectively at your situation to see if you are avoiding an obstacle. Constant effort is the best predictor of the completion of any long-term project.

13
Invisible Student

A dissertation is largely an independent endeavor that is characterized by guidance from a chair who oversees the process and progress that a student makes. Consequently, it is common for students to disappear unintentionally from the chair for long periods while they work on, and likely struggle with, various aspects of completion. Group and dyadic theories across a number of fields suggest that physical distance often leads to psychological distance, which in turn leads to apathy and feelings of annoyance when a time-intensive event or person pops up unexpectedly, usually at an inopportune time.

Like any professor, your chair is a busy professional, and unexpected events, such as illness, inclement weather, and even an unpredictable doctoral student, derails his/her progress with other responsibilities and projects. Although the dissertation is a doctoral student's priority, a chair has many priorities, so it is easy for a student to assume that the chair sees the importance or immediacy of the dissertation to the same degree as the student does. It is common for students to need or want a quick turnaround on a decision or approval, only to be frustrated by a chair's slow response or need to be reminded several times before he/she responds. It is also common for students and chairs to have mismatched enthusiasm, energy, and time when it comes to giving attention to a dissertation when contact between the two is sparse and infrequent. Without a way to monitor daily progress on a dissertation, your chair might interpret long periods between progress indicators as lack of effort, and in the extreme, abandonment of the dissertation. Circumstances can also change quickly, so frequent contact keeps both parties informed of the other's challenges. Richard recalls his disappearance from his chair:

When I started working on a particularly lengthy portion of my dissertation's data analysis, I worked week after week on tedious tasks. My chair and I discussed the time it would take for me to complete this section of analysis, but it took nearly 50%, or two months, longer than anticipated. I did not want to let my chair down, so I figured it was better to keep powering through the analysis and report to my chair when I was finished. As I neared the end of the analysis, I was surprised to receive an e-mail from my chair in which he stated that he was dissatisfied with my progress, and that I might need to extend the timeline for completion. He was gracious and understanding when I explained what had happened, but I learned an important lesson. Keep in contact with your chair, even if the news is unpleasant. Progress is progress no matter how slow, and you need to demonstrate that progress to your chair so that he/she does not interpret silence as stagnation.

Tiffany nearly jeopardized completion of her program when she disappeared:

My university had a 7-year do-or-die policy. During the 5th year of my program, I had been in little contact with my chair for nearly a year as I struggled with developing my proposal. At the beginning of the 6th year, I tried contacting my chair, but discovered that she was temporarily moved to an administrative position in the department while the incumbent recovered from an illness. She would still be my chair, but we both knew that her time was precious, and that would slow my progress with the dissertation. Progress was slow during the remainder of the 6th year, but I managed to graduate during the final semester before I reached the end of the do-or-die period. My advice to doctoral students is to remain visible to your chair during all parts of the dissertation. You never know what the future will bring, and it can only work against you.

Dissertations are lengthy projects that require completion and input from parties who often have competing demands, and when you disappear from your university, you risk perceptions of regression or apathy from your chair. No matter what challenges you face during your dissertation, remain in regular contact with your chair to avoid the psychological distance that manifests when people are separated for long periods. Don't treat your chair as a passive observer who is waiting patiently to hear from you.

14
It's Dangerous to Go Alone

If you are like most students, you will encounter areas of your dissertation that you cannot complete on your own. For example, most doctoral students have trouble emulating the type of scholarly writing required of them and that appears in scholarly journals, and so they engage a copyeditor to help them expose their dissertation's topic scholarly. Similarly, many doctoral students have trouble designing an empirical study that isolates the variables they are examining, and so they consult with experts on the subject to learn how to do it. Although some such help costs money, other help is just an office visit, phone call, or e-mail away.

New homeowners know, usually having found out the hard way, that if you have to go to the yellow pages or search the Internet for repair help after an incident occurs (e.g., broken water pipe, non-functioning breaker, leaky roof, etc.), it is too late. Therefore, it is prudent to know, at a minimum, a good plumber, electrician, and general contractor so you have someone to contact when things go wrong. The same is true during a dissertation, and so doctoral students should identify whom they will contact when they have trouble with their dissertations. Minimally, you should know a good copyeditor, statistician, and theorist in the field so you do not waste time, usually when it is most precious, when a problem is encountered. You should contact these people, introduce yourself, and let them know that you might need them later. This way you do not have to contact them cold when you are most in need of their help. Henri learned this lesson during his dissertation:

> After my dissertation was approved, I had to submit it to the university's graduate school for approval of the manuscript's format. The thesis office told me that I needed to make the text more scholarly before it could be approved. I tried to do so on my own, but after three iterations, I was told

that the office would not consider the manuscript again until I had the dissertation copyedited professionally. I needed to find a copyeditor who was familiar with copyediting dissertations, was familiar with my field, could copyedit my dissertation within three weeks so I could meet the thesis office's deadline, and wasn't too expensive so I could afford it. I asked around but found no one who could recommend a good copyeditor. I searched the Internet, but it was difficult to find a copyeditor who met the criteria above. I eventually found a copyeditor, but I went through a few stressful days thinking I might not ever find one.

Mason experienced a problem with statistics:

I muddled through the statistics in my dissertation, and everything was fine until my chair recommended that I add an analysis. I did not know how to conduct the analysis, which was especially difficult in my dissertation because I had used a multi-level model. I asked each of the professors I knew for help, but each was either too busy or unable to help with such an analysis. I consulted some books, but they did not address the multi-level issue I was facing. On a whim, I contacted the author of one of the books, and he was very generous with his time when helping me conduct the analysis. I had wasted about three weeks trying to deal with the issue on my own, but I figure that it was a cheap lesson that I would carry with me throughout my career and share with other students.

Whether applied to home ownership or dissertations, having help on standby is an excellent way to mitigate damage when you need help. Having to search for someone to help you wastes time and makes it more likely that you will have to settle for someone who will not be able to help you completely or to the degree that you need. Consider your abilities and the areas you will likely have problems with during your dissertation. Then, look for those people who can help you should the need arise. When you identify them, reach out to them to see if they will be available if and when you need them. If not, keep looking.

15
Is This a Game or Is It Real?

Most higher education, even in a doctoral program, occurs between a student and an instructor; rarely does a student's work (e.g., tests, grades, papers, etc.) go beyond the two. Most education is a simulation that mirrors real life, but that rarely has immediate consequences outside of the classroom. A dissertation is often a student's first experience with producing something that will go beyond an instructor because it is a contribution that is no longer for a fake audience. The fake audience is a concept so familiar to most students that they find it difficult to comprehend that a dissertation will be seen and judged by people beyond the dissertation committee.

Think back to the papers you wrote during your college studies. If you are like most students, you authored those papers to fulfill course requirements that an instructor created. Such papers demonstrated that learning had occurred, but in the larger picture, they had little effect on your life, and in just a few years, it won't matter much what grade you received for them. A dissertation is different because it transcends the classroom. Your dissertation will largely become a public document and a part of the literature that will be open to criticism by experts on the topic. A dissertation is not only a demonstration of learning or knowledge; it is a manuscript that a real audience will critique, criticize, praise, and possibly use to create more knowledge. Thomas forgot that his dissertation was not for a fake audience:

> While deciding on the instruments to use in my dissertation's model, I spent a long time heavily modifying an instrument because it was not created for use in my study's context. My chair was dissatisfied with what I had done, and she gave me two choices: 1) conduct a pilot study to validate the modified instrument, which would add about two months to my dissertation, or 2) find another measure that did not need to be modified.

I was angry with my chair because I could not see the difference. I chose the latter, and while I was discussing the choice with my chair, she told me why she had given me only two choices. Researchers in my field are especially leery of using invalidated instruments, and so although my modified instrument would have sufficed for the purposes of my dissertation, it would have been difficult to defend to other researchers, especially when I tried to publish findings from my study in a peer-reviewed journal. I am thankful to my chair for her foresight.

Theresa also forgot that the dissertation was not for a fake audience:

During my dissertation defense, one of my committee members did not like the way I had characterized use of a model that researchers in my field often use. I had stated that the model was used "nearly exclusively" across the field. The committee member showed me that my characterization was an overstatement, but I was resistant to change my characterization because it formed the basis of the purpose of the dissertation. I could not understand why that committee member was so insistent that I characterize the model's use so carefully. He required that I sample the literature and arrive at a percentage of researchers who used the model. The percentage was much lower than I had suggested, which reduced the importance of my dissertation's contribution. The committee member explained to me that I could not make such generalizations or guesses based on perception unless I had evidence of my claims. Hyperbole had no place in empirical research, and I could not use it to increase the importance of my study, especially since the truth was obtained so easily.

Dissertations serve a purpose beyond a classroom; they are real contributions to a field that might someday base future research. They must therefore be candid above all else. Given the experience doctoral students have with prior education, pedagogies, and programs, it is easy for them to forget that a dissertation is not something created for a fake audience. Although stressful to comprehend, a dissertation is an irrevocable document that other researchers, other than a chair and committee members, will critique, criticize, praise, and judge as a real contribution to a field.

16
Everyone's a Critic

The directions dissertations can take are infinite, making them wide open for criticisms that suggest where they are going, where they went, and where they should have gone. Most doctoral students embroiled in their dissertations receive unsolicited advice from many sources, even brothers, sisters, mothers, fathers, and strangers who have no experience conducting research. Luckily, most doctoral students are surrounded by people, at least while at the university, who have extensive research experience, but even veteran researchers disagree when it comes to how research should be conducted, which sends mixed messages to the student on how to proceed.

Whenever someone is working on a difficult project, it doesn't take long for observers to throw in their two cents, offering advice on all aspects of the project. Since it is impossible to employ all advice, especially since at least some of that advice will conflict, a person working on a project must learn to ignore, filter, or apply advice without losing sight of the purpose of the project. Entrepreneurs experience this phenomenon when starting a new business. Some people will tell the new business owner that it is a bad idea to start a business during such turbulent economic times, but then others will praise the entrepreneur for doing just that. Everyone is a critic, and it is common for people to offer conflicting, even paradoxical, advice. Doctoral students experience something similar from chairs and committee members, whose advice on how to proceed with a dissertation cannot be used simultaneously because it conflicts. Gregory received conflicting advice right from the start.

One of the first decisions that students who are conducting an empirical dissertation must make is whether to use a quantitative or qualitative design. I learned as much as I could about both, and after considering the state of the literature on my topic, I decided to proceed quantitatively. I was confident about my decision until I started receiving advice from several professors, both involved and not involved in my dissertation. One professor staunchly told me that a quantitative study was inappropriate for my dissertation given the state of the literature, and another, a member of my committee, insisted that a quantitative design was my only choice for the same reason. I received much advice that similarly conflicted throughout the dissertation. In the end, I realized that I needed to decide for myself what made sense, and pending my chair's approval, proceed with it confidently knowing that no study is perfect, and that not everyone would agree with what I did.

Olga's situation was similar:

I settled on a gap in the literature that I thought my dissertation would fill, and I presented my idea to two of my committee members who were both present during a meeting. One immediately voiced positive feedback on the topic I had chosen, but the other was opposed to it. Both began to provide advice on how I could improve the topic, and I tried my best to remember and record everything they said. During the next meeting with them, I showed them my latest proposal, in which I tried to incorporate all of the advice they had given me. It did not take long for my committee members to show me that what I was proposing was not only too ambitious, but that it was also impossible. I explained to them that I was just trying to incorporate all of their advice from the last meeting. They explained to me that everything they discussed with me last time was just that, a discussion to expose the weaknesses of the study and improve the topic. They never expected me to incorporate everything. They expected me to consider all that was said and improve the topic, knowing that I could not include everything.

Not all of the advice you will receive during your dissertation will be useful, and not all of it can be incorporated into a single study. As someone transitioning from student to independent researcher, you must weight all of your options and choose a topic, design, method, etc. that match the goals of the study. It is nearly certain that some of the advice you receive will be left on the cutting room floor.

17
I Would Like to Thank

Dissertations are far more social than most people perceive. Some professors consider dissertations to be the works of communities, not a single student. Consequently, most universities allow or require students to include an acknowledgments page in a dissertation to recognize those people, both academicians and others, who contributed to the dissertation in any way. However, during the hectic process that characterizes the dissertation, especially near the end when students experience the inevitable rush to finish, it is easy to forget either who deserves recognition for their contributions, or what each person added to the dissertation, making an acknowledgements page difficult to construct. This is especially true since the order of the acknowledgments often corresponds to the amount each person contributed.

Acknowledgements and academic manuscripts (e.g., dissertations, journal articles, conference papers, etc.) go hand-in-hand. It is common for researchers to recognize scholarly help, which ranges from casual conversations that result in the removal of a minor mistake to full reviews conducted during the journal review process. Most such recognition falls between unsubstantial aid (e.g., unskilled labor such as photocopying and printing) and a contribution that warrants authorship (e.g., construction of a model, data analysis, etc.). Most journals allow a section for authors to recognize such contributions to an article. Although doctoral students must author a dissertation alone, it is common for them to recognize the help and support they received from multiple people, including a spouse, family members, copyeditors, dissertation coaches, and professors, during the dissertation. At the very least, a student should thank the chair and committee members, but other people who deserve recognition are often mentioned on an acknowledgments page. Raymond's story is typical:

After the oral defense of the dissertation, I had only one week to submit my dissertation to the graduate office for final approval. Several sections were in disarray, including the citations and references, and the headings, tables, and figures. Those areas of the dissertation took priority because they represented major content areas of the document. At about 10:30 pm on the final night before I had to turn in the dissertation, I looked one more time at the university's dissertation template and I realized that I never wrote or included an acknowledgements page, which was required before the office would review the dissertation. To make matters worse, adding the page threw my pagination off, adding more time to format the dissertation that I didn't have. I hastily added the page, and after the dissertation was bound, I realized that I had forgotten to thank a major contributor to my dissertation. That person had walked me through the analysis portion of my dissertation, and I was embarrassed to have forgotten her, especially since I thanked other people who contributed much less than she did.

Shawna did something similar:

My dissertation ballooned to a 300-page document before I was done. Most of the bulk came from 90 tables that presented the results of the many analyses I conducted to answer my research questions. Consequently, many people contributed to my dissertation, and I was careful to list all of them in a file so I would not forget to recognize everyone who helped me. Although I was diligent with keeping that list, I forgot to include what each person contributed, and it was a mad rush just before graduation to try to remember how each person helped. In the end, I forgot a few people, mixed up who helped with what, and even spelled two people's names incorrectly. Given how intricate it was to construct the final document of my dissertation, especially since it contained so much material, it was a shame that the acknowledgements page, which appears near the front, contained so many errors.

Acknowledgments are more than good form. They prevent a researcher from taking full credit when some minor help that does not warrant authorship, but that requires recognition, contributed to the quality of a study or other publication, dissertations included. When things get busy near the end of your dissertation, you will be glad that you kept track of the people who helped you with it, and what each contributed.

18
Pygmalion Effect

Despite the stories, myths, and truths that surround the perception of how difficult dissertations are to complete, most students find that there were aspects of the dissertation that they enjoyed. Students who like solving puzzles often find the research design portion of the dissertation enjoyable, as do those who like writing when it comes to exposing their topic with prose. However, many students get caught up in the fun they found in the dissertation, and struggle to abandon it so they can proceed with their careers.

Students often find it difficult to let go of a dissertation, and therefore artificially extend it to keep tweaking it to strive for an unfulfillable goal. As students progress through a dissertation, they inevitably mature as researchers, and consequently, they begin to see areas of their studies that could have been better, or begin to revisit chapters that their chairs already approved. Some students take this to extreme and try to change entire sections or chapters, including core components such as research questions, hypotheses, and methods. The best chances a student has to complete a dissertation is to execute what was developed during the proposal and avoid allowing the dissertation to evolve. No contractor ever started building a small house and ended up building a mansion, and similarly, doctoral students should not try to improve the dissertation so that it no longer resembles the plan (i.e., proposal). Falling in love with the dissertation leads to the perception that perfection is the goal, and extends the time it takes to complete the dissertation, making it more likely that you will never finish, and less likely that the chair and committee will approve major deviations from the proposal. Norman fell in love with his dissertation, and almost failed to complete it as a result:

> I admit that I was a very inexperienced researcher at the beginning of my dissertation, and it is a wonder that I ever got my proposal approved. The

dissertation process was one of the most fascinating experiences of my life as I learned along the way to think objectively, develop theories, and use both to create new knowledge. I couldn't get enough of the process to the point of near obsession, and I often got sidetracked by imagining what the dissertation would look like if I changed its design, tested a different model, or used another sample of subjects. One of my committee members realized what I was doing, and commended me for my dedication and ability to see my dissertation from multiple viewpoints. However, he also reminded me that the proposal represented a type of contract that specified what I would deliver. He recommended that I stick to what the proposal said I would produce so that I could use my enthusiasm to conduct more studies as a professor after I graduated. I am a little embarrassed that my enthusiasm almost got the best of me.

Abigail's love for her dissertation created a stressful situation:

My dissertation's proposal was simple but elegant, and I truly believed that it would contribute significant findings to my field. However, as my dissertation progressed, I saw ways in which it could contribute even more, and I began adding analyses so that the dissertation became about 40 pages longer and bloated with 15 additional tables. When I submitted the dissertation to my chair, she was dismayed that I had deviated from the proposal so extensively, and she even called a special meeting with my committee to discuss the situation. I was lucky that all they had me do was remove the sections that the proposal did not call for. However, it was a stressful few days while I waited for the committee's verdict.

If you find the dissertation or some of its parts enjoyable, then you are likely suited to a life of research and scholarship. However, falling in love with a dissertation leads to perceptions of needing to produce perfection or more than the proposal required. Enthusiasm is a great motivator, but it can also prevent progress when experienced in abundance. If you follow your proposal, you are more likely to finish your dissertation, even if the dissertation ends up less than you know it could have been.

19
No-Brainer

If you are confused about what scholarly writing is, you are in good company because even professors who have years of experience with research sometimes do not fully understand the purpose or form of scholarly writing. After reading so many journal articles and other scholarly works that contain the type of writing that they which to emulate, it is surprising that students are unable to produce writing that is scholarly. The reason is because most people read for content, not structure, and if an author has done his/her job well, the exposition of a topic, which includes writing, conveys the content in a way that makes the conveyance invisible to the reader.

Many people assume that they know what scholarly writing is, and liken it, for example, to formal writing, in which topics are declared ceremoniously, or to sophisticated writing, which must be purposely esoteric. Others think that scholarly writing is measured objectively, and they use the grammar features of their word processors to assess the grade level at which they are writing. Some strive to write at the 19th or 20th grade levels or beyond (i.e., the perceived doctoral level), which makes prose read like stereo instructions. Both students and professors are surprised to discover that scholarly writing is much plainer than they imagined. As I teach to my copyediting clients, the hallmarks of scholarly writing are concision, clarity, accuracy, and reliability, which makes scholarly writing about expression, not impression. Julia's misperception of scholarly writing made it difficult for her to complete her dissertation:

> I didn't think much about the writing style I would use while writing my dissertation because I somehow thought that the writing would flow organically from me once I knew the topic I would be writing about. I was therefore surprised when I found it difficult to write even one coherent

sentence while trying to construct my literature review. At one point, I realized that I was trying to write as if I were the Queen of England, with much of my writing including words and phrases that I had never used before. I consulted a copyeditor, and he told me that I was trying to write above my capacity, which means I was making everything in the chapter—every word, every sentence, every concept—sound important, or dissertation-worthy. He suggested that I just write normally and stop trying to conform to the perceptions of scholarly writing I held. It was still difficult, but at least I stopped trying to impress my chair and committee, and other readers, with something at which I was poor.

Gabe's misperceptions about scholarly writing took another form:

I was unsure about what writing should look like in a dissertation, but I assumed that it should look like the kind of writing found in peer-reviewed journals. The problem was that I did not know how to write about a topic and simultaneously make the words I chose scholarly. So, I used my word processor's built-in thesaurus to change the vocabulary to make my writing seem more scholarly. When I submitted my second chapter to my chair, he was dissatisfied with the writing, and he suggested that I hire a copyeditor. My copyeditor informed me that scholarly writing is not a function of vocabulary. Using scholarly vocabulary in sentences structured unscholarly is like placing the hood ornament from a luxury car on a common car; it just doesn't match, and only draws attention to a writer's inability to write scholarly. It turns out that my standard writing style sufficed as scholarly writing, but I wish I knew that before I tried making my writing artificially more scholarly.

Scholarly writing is not about formality, sophistication, or impression. It is about exposing a topic candidly by adhering to hallmarks that make writing accessible to readers. Misperceptions and assumptions about scholarly writing are common causes of writer's block, and time spent rewriting chapters to convert writing to something that matches what is found in journals. If you are confused about what scholarly writing is, find a few well-written articles in a top journal in your field, but instead of reading them for content, read for the construction of the text. You will be surprised just how plain and straight-forward scholarly writing is.

20
Magret de Canard on a Soiled Platter

Trying to do two things at once is always more difficult than trying to do either alone. Doctoral students often place themselves into a situation of having to do two things at once when it comes to writing and developing the content for a dissertation. Trying to build a shed while simultaneously learning how to cut wood means that the shed will likely be less than it could have been. Similarly, learning to write scholarly while trying to compose a dissertation results in less-than-desirable exposition of the topic. One of the most powerful things a student can do to prepare for a dissertation is learning how to write scholarly.

Writing is part science and part art. The science side of writing is evident in the ways grammar, parts of speech, and the rules that define them combine to convey meaning to a reader. The art side of writing distinguishes one type of writing from another, which is why poems and sonnets look so different from instructions on how to operate a machine. Scholarly writing largely has to do with exposing a topic candidly, and there are rules and heuristics that guide such candidness. If you do not already know how to write scholarly before you begin writing your dissertation, you will be facing two fronts—having to learn how to write scholarly and having to produce scholarly writing. Such trial-by-fire elevates the probability that you will not only struggle to produce the chapters of your dissertation, but also that you will be unable to finish the dissertation. Laura's experience with scholarly writing is common among doctoral students:

> Whenever I began writing my dissertation, I had no idea how to say what I was thinking. I would struggle for hours just to write a few sentences, and this went on for days and weeks at a time. I shared my inability to get any significant writing done with my chair, and she suggested that I step away from the dissertation and immerse myself in scholarly writing. She

suggested a few books on the topic, and that I should consult with the on-campus writing coach, whom I did not know existed. Although I was hardly an expert at writing by the time I returned to my dissertation, I had learned some techniques that helped me get some writing done, which could be edited later. As I progressed from chapter to chapter, I found that writing became increasingly easier. I never thought that I would first have to learn how to write before I could write the chapters of my dissertation.

Samuel had trouble writing for a different reason:

While writing the literature review chapter of my dissertation, I didn't think clearly about how I was going to justify my hypotheses. I wrote in a compartmentalized fashion; I cited evidence from the literature but failed to synthesize that evidence into coherent arguments. I created what my dissertation coach called a literature pile, where I would write, "This author found this and that author found that, and here is a hypothesis related to those findings." I was not considering how the evidence from the literature led logically to my hypotheses. I had to take a break from writing to learn how to write a dissertation. It was time well spent because the same type of writing appears in journals, and I intended to become a professor and researcher after I graduated. However, it took me longer to finish my dissertation as a result, and I found out the hard way that learning how to write while trying to produce quality writing is almost impossible. My advice to future doctoral students is to learn how to write before you start writing your dissertation.

Scholarly writing is not something picked up easily along the way, and having to learn how to write a dissertation and write it at the same time leads to wasted time, frustration, and possibly an unfinished dissertation. I know of many cases in which failure to know how to write scholarly nearly cost students their doctoral degrees. Don't face two fronts at the same time. Learn to write scholarly before you need to produce scholarly writing.

21
Judging a Horse by Its Saddle

The thought of producing a book-length manuscript is frightening. Students commonly cannot imagine writing the amount of text that a dissertation requires, and most have trouble doing it. There isn't anything that anyone can do to reduce the amount of writing that a dissertation contains because they are comprehensive, lengthy, and prolix contributions to a field. Consequently, students see them as insurmountable, and even society and media use the term *dissertation* hyperbolically to suggest a lengthy or excessive amount of text (e.g., "I asked him to write just a few paragraphs and he wrote a whole dissertation").

What image comes to your mind when you think of a dissertation? If you are like most doctoral students, you think of a thick, large-format book with a leather or vinyl cover, perhaps adorned with gilded lettering. The thickness of a dissertation scares most people, but by the time a dissertation's front matter, references, tables, figures, appendices, etc. are removed, about 90 pages of text remain, or about 27,000 words at an average of 300 words per page. This means that if you wrote just 3 pages a day, or about 900 words, which is about twice the length of the average journal abstract, you could be finished with writing your dissertation in just 30 days. It doesn't take 12, 18, or even 24 months or more to *write* a dissertation, it takes that long to *conduct* a dissertation. The reason students struggle with a dissertation's text is because they usually sit down to write without a plan or outline to guide them. Rita's experience with writing her dissertation is common among doctoral students:

> My chair asked me to begin by writing the methods chapter first to determine whether my dissertation's design was viable and would answer my research questions. On my first day of writing, I stared blankly at my laptop's screen for about an hour because I had no idea how to begin. I

looked to other dissertations for help, but they showed me only how to structure the chapter, not fill it with original content. I had assumed that the chapter would come together on its own as I added content to its pages, but without considering what content to add and in what order it should appear, I had no idea where to begin. I learned that the same was true for the other chapters as I tried to write them later. Creating a very detailed outline for each chapter was essential to avoid having to make up the writing as I went along.

Paulo also had trouble writing his dissertation:

I thought hard about how to structure my literature review so that it contained all of the parts I wanted to include, but also so that it was long enough to serve as a literature review for a dissertation. I began by creating the headings that I wanted the chapter to contain, and I calculated the average number of words I needed to add under each heading to make the chapter the length I thought I needed it to be. I began filling in the text under the headings, and I was pleased when I had about 10,000 words. However, my chair told me that I would have to restructure the content I had written into arguments, and not just have never-ending strings of citations and transitional sentences. I had failed to construct arguments in the chapter, and instead had just filled it with content according to the headings I had created.

An outline of a dissertation is like a schematic. It should be detailed enough so that you can see the major sections of the chapter (i.e., headings), the arguments contained under them (i.e., combinations of findings from the literature), and the evidence that supports them (i.e., individual findings from the literature). Then you can see how the entire chapter will look once written. Once you are satisfied with a chapter's outline, it should simply be a matter of putting it into paragraph form. If you sit down in front of your computer and you are unsure of what to write about, you are not ready to write. Rethink the dissertation's content, and return to writing when ready.

22
Right Answer, Wrong Question

The bound edition of a dissertation belies the blood, sweat, and tears that went into creating it. Students who reminisce about what went into creating a dissertation are often disappointed that the result is so much smaller than expected. Doctoral students often fall into the trap of thinking that a chapter should mirror the time, effort, expense, etc. that went into creating it. For example, students often spend months researching designs, choosing a design, creating a model, finding subjects to participate, and collecting data, and yet the methods chapter, the one that contains all of these components, is often one of the shortest in the dissertation.

The dissertation is an experience of both learning and self-discovery because it represents a transformational process for the student, but in the end, the dissertation needs to contain only a contribution to a field, not a record of the student's personal journey. It is common for students to discuss the painstaking steps they took to collect data, or the tremendous manual effort they endured while analyzing data. Some even go so far as to brag about the time they spent on a portion of the dissertation, usually to impress the reader, garner sympathy, or demonstrate due diligence. This occurs because the mood an author is in while writing affects the text that he/she produces. It is difficult to spend weeks collecting and analyzing data, or scouring the literature to find a gap to fill, to produce only a few sentences for the effort. Cathy's story demonstrates this phenomenon:

> My dissertation's literature review required me to be comprehensive with literature searches to ensure that I had considered all articles that pertained to the topic of my study. I would often spend 4 to 5 days searching for, reading, and assessing articles found from a single search term, and the result was the listing of a few articles in a table that took about 5 minutes to create. When reporting the process I used to search for the

articles, I went into great detail about the time I spent online, the time I spent at my and other universities' libraries, and even the hours per day I spent conducting the searches. My chair told me that the searches were simply a part of the process necessary to conduct the study I chose to conduct, and that I needed to discuss them more scholarly before she would approve the chapter.

Chad took the practice to extreme:

Collection of data during my dissertation was particularly arduous because I simultaneously had to consider the subjects, the timing of the collection, and the level at which the data were collected. The process was so difficult to deal with, that if I had to go back and do it again, I would choose another design or even another topic to avoid it. I must have been in states of exhaustion, anger, and euphoria when I wrote the methods chapter of my dissertation because I packed in quite a number of colloquialisms, idioms, and oxymorons to describe the process. I don't know whether I was trying to impress everyone or express my anger toward the process, but the result was a ridiculous exposition of the methods I used to collect my data. I was lucky that I didn't get too far before a fellow student saw what I was doing and recommended that I reconsider my approach to writing. I did, and I am thankful that someone was around to clue me in to my mistake.

To be blunt, no one cares about the personal journey you endured to conduct your dissertation. What you generally did to finish your dissertation is what all students who came before you did to complete theirs. Your dissertation was extraordinary to you, but was common in your field. The key here is to remember who your audience is because the readers of your dissertation have likely seen it all before, and you are unlikely to impress them. The purpose of the dissertation manuscript is to report the study, not evoke readers' emotions. Choose wisely the exposition you use to report the journey you endured during your dissertation, and ensure that it matches the scholarly tone that your readers expect from you.

23
False Positive

Professors, and especially researchers who are experts on the same topic, are known well for using jargon and inside uses of words and phrases that deviate from common use such that it takes tacit knowledge about a field to be able to speak their language. Being able to speak the language of a field is a sign of indoctrination, seniority, or membership within it. Since students are still novices in their fields, they often misinterpret and misuse their field's jargon. This especially pertains to jargon associated with research methods, the portion of their studies with which students struggle most.

Minor misuse, or failure to use, jargon by students is forgivable since they are still novice researchers, but such misuse works against a student because it signals novice status, making it more difficult for people, especially chairs and committee members, to see the student as a peer, or someone who is transitioning from student to independent researcher. Speaking a language is a strong signal that a person belongs among those who speak it fluently. Consequently, it is paramount that a student be able to use jargon correctly in both speech and writing, and avoid trying to use jargon until its use is understood fully. Learning to use scholarly jargon correctly is a matter of experience; nowhere does a dictionary of scholarly jargon exist for each field. You need to pick it up from contact with your professors, journal articles, books, and other sources by being immersed in your field. If there were one rule when it comes to scholarly jargon, it is don't use a word or phrase until you are certain of its meaning, and never try to sound scholarly in either speech or writing by throwing around jargon you do not understand. Teri's incorrect use of scholarly jargon caused her some embarrassment:

I was conducting a phenomenological qualitative study for my dissertation, and during my search for qualitative studies on my topic, I noticed that the same terms kept popping up again and again. I especially saw the words *in-depth* and *saturation* appear repeatedly in qualitative studies. Wanting the writing in my dissertation to be scholarly, I used these terms often since I thought it was the norm in studies that used qualitative designs. It turned out that I was using the terms both incorrectly and too frequently, and my chair rejected one of my chapters multiple times because of it. I suspect that she was beginning to question whether I knew what I was talking about, and that I might be simply going through the motions of conducting my study through mimicry. I realized that I had better learn how to use those words correctly, and a few conversations with more experienced researchers set me straight.

Nick's misapplication of jargon was more serious:

I never realized that a single word could cause so much trouble until I began writing my dissertation. The subjects of my study were solicited over e-mail, and they self-selected to participate by showing up to a laboratory over the course of several days. To avoid several biases, the subjects were assigned randomly into one of two conditions when they arrived. I erroneously referred to this method as *random* assignment. What I did not realize was that I had suggested that the subjects were chosen randomly from the population, and that self-selection for participation was not a feature of the study. My chair halted my progress and made me write a short paper on the meaning of random assignment, and the difference between what it means and what I was doing in my study. It was a hard lesson to learn, but one that I will not forget when it comes to the words I choose when writing up a study.

Proper use of jargon within a group signals membership, and likewise, misuse of and failure to use jargon similarly signals nascence or outsider status. When writing and discussing your dissertation, you do not want to signal such nascence to people you are trying to convince that you are making, or have made, a transition from outsider to insider (i.e., from student to independent researcher). Before you start throwing your field's jargon into speech and writing, ensure that you are using it correctly.

24
You Know What They Say

All researchers face pressures to make what they are researching sound important, especially to satisfy the *filling a gap in the literature* and *contributing to the literature* goals that are required to advance both doctoral programs and careers. Unfortunately, many researchers forget (or never learned) that a researcher does that by demonstrating the importance of research, not creating it. Here, research shares some similarities with journalism; a journalist's job is to report the news, not create it through sensationalizing—what is called *yellow journalism* in that field.

Sensational copy is common in our culture; advertisers are especially known to use hyperbolic descriptors and indefinite statements (e.g., "up to 99% effective") to entice buyers. The adage *caveat emptor* (i.e., let the buyer beware) is not only wise, but necessary to survive the overload. A similar situation occurs in research, but when it comes to dissertations, the adage *caveat venditor* (i.e., let the seller beware) is more appropriate. In essence, you need to be careful what you write (i.e., sell) because it will be scrutinized in greater detail than you can imagine, and you will be accountable for what you claim. However, pressures to produce research that fills a gap cause doctoral students to use weasel words and arguments to suggest importance where no evidence of it exists. Such arguments occur when authors discuss a topic's importance but do not demonstrate the source of that importance, and when they attribute ideas to theoretical third parties who are never discussed. These practices violate the candidness principle that guides research in all fields, and goes against the hallmarks of scholarly writing. Yosef was unaware that he was using weasel words in his dissertation:

> I was not confident about the content of my dissertation, but not knowing how to convey it in writing meant that I was fighting two things at the

same time. Eventually, my chair recommended that I talk to a writing coach. I did, and the coach showed me, among other things, that my writing was filled with weasel words, phrases, and arguments. I used phrases like "researchers argue that…" and "much research suggests that…," but I never followed such statements with citations. As my coach said, I was forcing the reader to just trust me that such statements were accurate. A rewrite by me and a copyedit by a professional editor made my dissertation both more scholarly and acceptable to my chair and committee.

Millicent also used weasel words in her dissertation:

I chose a topic for my dissertation that offered little literature from which to draw. I often found myself having to justify my topic based on little empirical evidence and occasional leaps of faith. My dissertation was full of exaggerations and weasel arguments. For example, I found a measure for a variable that appeared only once in the literature. The measure consisted of 4 sub-dimensions, and the article that used the measure reported reliability coefficients of 0.56, 0.67, 0.69, and 0.78, meaning that three of them failed to demonstrate adequate reliability (i.e., 0.7). In my dissertation, I used the phrase "can reach 0.78" when describing those reliabilities. My chair found this unacceptable, and one of my committee members told me that I had tried to hide poor results by reporting only the highest value and passing the measure off as acceptable. In other words, I had made a weasel argument by not including all relevant information.

Pressures to make scholarly writing (such as that found in dissertations) sound important cause many authors to engage in tactics found in other types of writing. The most common tactic is using weasel words, which often expands into weasel arguments. Claims, arguments, propositions, and hypotheses must be supported by literature; they must be verifiable beyond simply reassurance from the author. As an author of scholarly manuscripts, you need to be especially careful not to use theoretical third parties and statements that hide the truth to make your claims sound bigger or more important than they are. Essential here is demonstrating the importance of a topic, not creating it. If you can't do the former, you need to either research the topic more, or find a new one.

25
Exit Stage Left

Researchers commonly second-guess their own research, agonizing over whether a method chosen was the best alternative, hypotheses are argued well, and results are sufficiently strong to warrant publication. It is therefore unsurprising that scholarly writers try to limit their exposure to criticism, fault, and failure by using language in their writing that removes the author from the author's own choices, arguments, findings. The result is prose that is weak and that does not convey a tone of confidence. Some authors even go so far as to apologize for their choices, engaging in a mild form of self-deprecation in their writing, and the more inexperienced the author, the more limiting the language.

Authors who use limiting language in their writing to deflect blame, criticism, or fault are engaging in hedging, usually in the form of vague, noncommittal, and ambiguous language that makes it difficult for a reader to know who is making a claim, reporting a finding, or responsible for a thought. The most common signs of hedging are using auxiliary verbs (e.g., "Variable A might correlate with Variable B"), attributing arguments to theoretical third parties (e.g., "One could argue that…" and "It can be argued that…"), and using limiting qualifiers (e.g., "Managers often/usually/sometimes use leadership to…"). Even the subjunctive mood acts as a hedge (e.g., "Variable A should correlate with Variable B"). Occasional use of hedging is natural, but overuse creates writing that is difficult to read and accept; if an author is unsure of his/her arguments, methods, and findings, how can the reader be? Donald found himself hedging while writing his dissertation:

> The weakest chapter in my dissertation was the methodology chapter. I admit that I began writing the chapter before I was ready, and I learned that as a result, I had included a lot of hedging language in the chapter. At every turn, every argument, every statement, I allowed too much room

for backpedaling in case someone found fault with or criticized my writing and the content it conveyed. I made the mistake of writing the chapter especially for the limited audience of my chair and committee, and I failed to emulate the writing found in the best journals in my field. In the end, I hired a copyeditor to remove the hedging from the chapter, and I was amazed at how much better the writing was after the edit.

Barb also had a problem with hedging while writing her dissertation's proposal:

During our doctoral programs, my cohorts and I had it drilled into us that our research would never "prove" anything, and that we were only adding to the conversation on a topic, not putting any theory, relationship, or finding to rest. I took that lesson to the extreme, ensuring that any topic I wrote about in my proposal allowed room for doubt. I found out later that I was using hedging in my writing to remain what I thought was objective. However, it turns out that I was exposing the topic of my dissertation with too much ambiguity and uncertainty. Imagine if you took the blueprints to a house and randomly added a few inches here and there to make room for imperfections during construction. Those few inches here and there would add up to a disproportioned house. The same is true in writing; a little room for doubt is alright if used sparingly, but if you use it to hedge every aspect of the dissertation's content, it adds up to disproportioned and poorly written research.

Some crafty writers use hedging purposely so that they are able to backpedal if an argument, recommendation, or conclusion is later found faulty. This is especially true for research that appears in print, an irrevocable medium. Students typically have it easier because dissertations are scrutinized by multiple pairs of eyes, and are reworded and reworked, until an acceptable version is produced. The most common cause of hedging in writing is discomfort with a topic. If you find yourself uncomfortable writing about any aspect of the dissertation, don't continue writing until you are comfortable. Otherwise, you will be compelled to qualify, hedge, and limit every aspect of the writing to avoid being criticized or found at fault by your chair or committee.

26
Me, Myself, and I

When choosing a field to study at the doctoral level, most students select one that is personally interesting, or one to which the student believes he/she can contribute over a lifetime of study. It is therefore understandable that some of the passion that drives a student to a field leaks into his/her writing, especially a dissertation. When justifying studying a topic for a dissertation, students commonly expose personal motives, experiences, and feelings, and include judgmental language, to espouse a topic, making it appear that the topic was not pursued objectively.

Editorials offer opinions, provide an opposing viewpoint, and discuss a topic without needing to provide evidence or proof of conclusions. From that description, it is clear that editorials, or language that resembles an editorial, should not appear in a dissertation. Even research that uses emic designs retains objectivity. The two most common areas students use editorial language are in a dissertation's justification and its results. While justifying the dissertation—that is, answering the question "Why did you conduct this study?"—students often cite personal reasons, not realizing that the question is really asking "Why should this study become part of the conversation in this field?" Some chairs, committees, and even universities either dissuade or disallow students from using the first person (i.e., "I" and "we") to steer the student away from editorial claims. Similarly, students often demonstrate the importance of their findings by using language that exaggerates or diminishes them, depending on which direction is most advantageous to the student. The result is editorial language. Brian ran into this problem early during his dissertation:

> My university required me to explicitly explain why I was conducting my dissertation, but I misinterpreted the question, and instead provided a background that included my experiences with the topic. I explained that

the topic was important to me, and that I wanted to study it to help people who were in a similar situation. My chair pointed out that the question was asking me to explain how the study contributed to the literature, and justify the study's inclusion in it. Luckily, I got it right the second time around, and I learned a lesson in how to interpret the questions I needed to answer in the dissertation.

Paige had a problem with the language she used in her dissertation:

> To be honest, the results I got for my dissertation were both weak and disappointing. Many of the tests I performed for the hypotheses were barely non-significant (e.g., $p=0.052$), and those that were significant were barely under the line (e.g., $p=0.047$). Two tests suggested negative relationships, though I hypothesized positive correlations. When I got to the discussion of results chapter, I started to creatively (as my chair put it) discuss my findings in a positive light. I talked about how unfortunate it was that I got results so close to the p-value's cutoff, and how surprising it was that positively hypothesized relationships were found to be negative. I even went so far as to blame the literature for not finding a similar result. When I turned the discussion chapter in to my chair, she rejected it, and I spent about 6 weeks rewriting it.

Passion invites strong language when writing about a topic, and pressure to demonstrate the importance of research leads to judgmental and exaggerated descriptions, the two most common sources of editorial language. While writing a dissertation, avoid language that either indicates or suggests judgement. Be especially careful of words such as *unfortunately* and *surprisingly* (e.g., "Unfortunately, H1 was not supported" and "Surprisingly, the coefficient was negative"). Such words suggest that the findings, though not hypothesized, are as valuable as if the hypotheses were supported. Limit the first person (i.e., "I" and "we") to statements that allow you to avoid overuse of the passive voice (e.g., "I argue that…"), and avoid it when discussing justifications for the study (e.g., "I chose this topic because…"). With a little practice, removing judgmental and emotional appeals—language found in editorials—will become second nature during scholarly writing.

27
Chronology Crisis

Since the content and exposition in dissertations are revised, revisited, and rewritten, the dissertation is much more of a major project than a study. As I've said to all of my dissertation coaching clients, the dissertation is like nothing you've ever done, and like nothing you will ever do again, and most of my clients agree. This is a problem for students who are disorganized or often fall behind in the administration of a dissertation, or who are accustomed to keeping track of a project in their heads. The result is commonly an extended program, and uncommonly the incompletion of it.

Most people do not have formal training on project management. The usual advice that goes along with completing a lengthy project, such as setting a schedule, keeping good records, and taking breaks occasionally, applies to dissertations, but most people are unaccustomed to working on projects as complex, lengthy, and confusing as dissertations, and the experience is universally overwhelming. One of the most unanticipated aspects of the dissertation is how many times an argument, section, or chapter will be revisited and revised before a final version is arrived at. Some revisitations continue to occur right up to the eleventh hour, which is one of the reasons that dissertations end so abruptly; it seems that one minute the chair judges the dissertation inadequate, and then suddenly, after just one more revision, he/she accepts it as complete. Veronica's experiences demonstrate that multiple revisitations can cause problems for students who are unprepared:

> I wrote the methods chapter of my dissertation with as much care as I could, but my chair rejected it, telling me that I should try using another method to collect and analyze my data. I made the mistake of simply revising the original version I sent to her, rather than copying the text to a new file so I could keep the original intact. When I showed my chair the new version, she rejected it and told me to return to the original. The

problem was that I no longer had a copy of the original because I had edited it to create the most recent version. I spent nearly a month trying to recreate the original version of the chapter, and I even had to ask my chair about a few of the details, and about some of the citations I had used, because I could not remember exactly what it had contained. From that moment on, I kept and dated each version of everything I wrote so that I could turn back the clock on any part my dissertation at any moment.

Anthony's experiences echo the need for proper management of a dissertation's manuscript:

I was careful to label each version of my dissertation in each file's name, and I even kept a log to identify changes made to the dissertation at each iteration. Unfortunately, I tended to create a new version—nearly every day—each time I worked on it, so I ended up with hundreds of versions, each of which contained only small changes from the previous version. Since I worked on the dissertation out of sequence, it was difficult to figure out which version contained which changes, and I often found myself combining changes from one file with those from another. It became a nightmare trying to keep track of what was where, especially when it came to the references. I realize now that I should not have created a new file each time I worked on the dissertation, but instead decided subjectively when a new version was warranted. Perhaps weekly would have been a better choice, or each time my chair approved something.

Project management skills aid students who are embarking on a dissertation, but lacking such skills, students apply their experiences with managing small projects to the dissertation, and discover later that large projects require a different set of skills. Before beginning your dissertation, create a plan for managing the document that represents the dissertation, and be prepared for the many inevitable revisions that characterize lengthy projects, especially dissertations. Decide how you will measure milestones and manage the content of your dissertation using those milestones, and be flexible enough to change both as the dissertation unfolds.

28

Obvious Mismatch

Some universities, departments, and chairs require students to follow a standard in their dissertations when it comes to citations and references (e.g., APA, MLA, CMS), but some allow students to choose the standard based on the content of the dissertation and the field being studied. When given a choice, students commonly choose the standard that top journals in their fields use. The problem is that many journals use proprietary standards, or modify better-known standards to meet the needs of the journal. Many journals are known for stating that they require one standard for submission but then give examples that don't match that standard. The result is frustration for both students and researchers.

From a purely pragmatic viewpoint, the best standard to choose is one that is easy to implement (i.e., not overly complex when it comes to formatting citations and references), covers all types of references that students include in their dissertations (e.g., journal articles, books, dissertations, conference papers, etc.), and is well-documented (e.g., printed in book form for easy reference). Standards that meet these criteria are easy to find, but students often choose their citation and referencing standards for other reasons, and get themselves into trouble consequently. In my experience as a dissertation coach, most students discount the importance of choosing the right standard, usually because they think of formatting citations and references as a menial task, or because they think that they can deal with it later once the dissertation is written, a seemingly more important task at the beginning of a dissertation. Yvette discovered that using the wrong criteria during selection of a citation and referencing standard can waste time:

> My university required me to choose a referencing standard for my dissertation that a journal in my field uses. I knew that one particular journal would be cited in my dissertation often, and that I wanted to one day

publish my dissertation in that journal, so I figured that choosing that journal as a referencing standard made sense. I soon realized the mistake I had made in choosing that journal because it was proprietary, and it did not include examples of how to cite and reference some types of sources such as conference papers, dissertations, websites, and videos. Nearly all citations and references in the journal were journal articles and books. I figured that I could then make up my own standard to cite those uncommon sources. My chair did not allow it, and I was forced mid-dissertation to choose another standard. I will never forget the three weeks I spent reformatting all of my citations and references.

James found that a mismatch between a citation and referencing standard and the content of a dissertation can be costly:

It is common for finance papers, and dissertations on financial topics, to include lengthy footnotes that take the reader off on tangents. There is much material in an empirical finance paper that an author must acknowledge, even if it does not pertain directly to the current topic. Unfortunately, I made the mistake of choosing a citation standard that uses footnotes, so I ended up with about 800 references and footnotes when I finished writing the dissertation. The footnotes on some pages were so long that they spanned multiple pages. The reader had to flip forward a page or two to finish reading the footnote and then flip back to continue reading the main text. In the end, my chair and I decided to use another referencing standard, and it took nearly two months to reformat the document to the new standard.

Nothing is trivial in a document as lengthy as a dissertation. Even something as seemingly simple as page numbering can prove difficult and cumbersome, so when it comes to citations and references—a portion of the dissertation that comprises 25% to 30% of its length—choosing the standard is crucial. Base your decision not on a top journal's use of a standard or something to do with your career goals (e.g., publishing in a certain journal). Choose a standard that matches the format of your dissertation and is well-documented so you have a source to cite in case someone (e.g., your chair or a committee member) challenges your use of the standard.

29
Prep Standards

While working on a dissertation, students focus on identifying a gap in the literature, deciding on a research design, analyzing data, writing up results, and gaining the approval of a chair and committee. It is therefore common for students to ignore what they perceive to be minor details, including formatting the dissertation's document and ensuring that supplements such as tables, figures, and appendices conform to the standards that the university and chair require. As is the case with most dissertations, students are often rushing when the conclusion of the dissertation approaches, and that's when the details add up to create both minor and major crises.

Doctoral students wear many hats while working on a dissertation—those of researcher, project manager, secretary, analyst, statistician, author, negotiator, etc.—and the ability to switch hats, and wear more than one at the same time, is crucial to a dissertation's completion. It is therefore common for students to push less important tasks into the future to work on more immediate ones in the present. However, unless students return to those less-important tasks at some time during the dissertation, they pile up and must be addressed near the end, a stage when time is short. This is usually when students find that the preparatory standards that the university requires are difficult, if not impossible, to adhere to. Sophia experienced this problem when it came to a table:

Most of my dissertation relied on the creation of a very large table that summarized findings in the literature. The table was not only large, it was also complex, containing many merged cells that made alteration of the widths and heights of the columns and rows difficult; changing the size of one column or row made the content of some of the cells difficult to read. I was relieved when the table was completed near the beginning of my dissertation, and I did not alter it for months during the remainder of the study. After my dissertation defense, I had just one task left—format the

57

document to the university's requirements and submit it to the thesis office for approval. The problem is that I created the table using 1-inch margins, and the thesis office required 1.5 inches for the left margin and 1.25 for the top, right, and bottom. The table didn't fit on a page with those margins, and since I was not allowed to use a font smaller than 10 point, it was not simply a matter of changing the font size. I had to reconstruct the entire table, and it took so long, that I nearly missed the cutoff date to graduate during that semester.

Jackson experienced a similar problem with formatting paragraphs:

I made the mistake of not reading the university's dissertation and thesis formatting rules before I started writing my dissertation, and so I was unaware of a strange formatting requirement. No paragraph in a dissertation was allowed to have more than 8 sentences. Even my chair was unaware of this rule. When it came time to format the document, I found myself having to place paragraph breaks in weird places, and sometimes I even had to add filler sentences in places where I had just one or two sentences in a paragraph at the end of a section or chapter. Splitting up the paragraphs also wreaked havoc on the placement of my tables and figures, and even created problems with placement of section headings. It took a long time to complete the formatting of my dissertation. I should have familiarized myself with the rules before I started writing.

During any large project, it is common to ignore seemingly low-priority tasks to concentrate on what's important at the moment, but details can sneak up on you when you least expect it. Formatting intuitively occurs at the end when the dissertation is complete. However, knowing the preparatory standards before beginning a dissertation saves time at the end, the stage during which students are rushing to make last-minute changes to the content of a dissertation, preparing for the defense, and dealing with other tasks left to the end, including checking citations and references, and confirming data analyses. The aphorism *look before you leap* applies well to the formatting of a dissertation.

30
Ten Thousand Clicks

A tool is only as useful as the person who wields it, and it is the poor artisan who blames his/her tools. Consequently, the more you know about how to use a tool, and the more experience you have using it, the better the product will be. Doctoral students use many tools to conduct a study associated with a dissertation, including literature databases, statistics programs, and word processors. The last one gets more students into trouble than you think, especially since most people, doctoral students included, consider themselves proficient with word processors simply because they use them so often.

Next only to Web browsers and e-mail programs, word processors are the most commonly used software on personal computers. They are so common, using them daily leads people to believe that they can use all functions that word processors offer. The truth is that most users are aware of only a word processor's most basic functions. While creating a book-length document during a dissertation, students use many more of a word processor's functions. Most dissertations include a table of contents that uses leader tabs, references with hanging indents, and numbering that differs based on pagination. Being familiar only with a word processor's basic functions means that such advanced features must be learned at the same time that they are being applied. Li learned just how much time can be wasted when a user is unaware that a word processor has advanced formatting functions:

> The references standard used in my dissertation required what I later learned are hanging indents. I thought I had to do it manually, so I used a series of line breaks and 5 spaces to make all lines after the first indented for each reference. With over 300 references, it felt like I had clicked my mouse and pushed the spacebar about 10,000 times to format the references. When I turned in the final version of my dissertation for approval,

I learned from an editor that word processors can create hanging indents automatically. I cut and pasted the references from an earlier version of the dissertation into the current version, and simply used the word processor's indentation tool to create the hanging indents. When I think of the hours I spent doing it manually, I realize that I should have searched the Internet for an easier way to do it.

Lucas had a similar problem with indentation:

The first line of all paragraphs in my dissertation had to be indented, even for paragraphs following a section heading. I used the tab key on the keyboard to create those indents, but I later learned that the university requires indents to be created using the word processor's indentation feature. The reason is that XML, the language used to create electronic copies of a document, cannot interpret tabs from a document created in a word processor. I had my work cut out for me because my dissertation contained hundreds of tabbed indents. I changed all the tabbed indents by hand, and after about 4 hours, one of my cohorts asked what I was doing. After I explained, she showed me how to make the word processor do the change for me. She did in about 10 seconds what I hadn't accomplished in hours. I admit that I was not a wizard when it came to using the word processor, but I should have asked around for a better way to do it.

A word processor is the tool you'll use most during your dissertation, so it is wise to learn its advanced features before beginning to write. Nearly all labor-intensive tasks can be automated in contemporary word processors, you just have to know how to do it. For example, you can ask a word processor to search for all text in a certain font and change the font of that text to another. You can even have a word processor search for and identify paragraph breaks, page breaks, section breaks, white space, footnotes, and endnote marks, which are abundant in lengthy manuscripts. Anything is easy when you know how to do it, and knowing more than the basics when it comes to word processing will make your experience with your dissertation more pleasant and less time-consuming.

31
Close Enough

Formatting citations and references is tedious, and they interrupt the flow of writing when an author must add a citation to the text and then subsequently add it to the references at the end of a document. It is common for authors to lose their train of thought when they do this, and it shows up in their writing in the form of questionable grammar, repetition of content, and incoherent arguments. This is especially problematic during dissertations because they are lengthy and the number of citations and references makes formatting unwieldy. The situation is exacerbated when a student is unfamiliar with citation and referencing standards.

Most formatting of citations and references harkens to the days of pre-digital, pre-word processor print standards that have long since become outdated. They persist because standards die hard, and most publishers of such standards are reluctant to change long-standing, well-known institutions of publishing. Does it really matter if a period or comma appears here or there in a citation, and what would happen were an author's first and middle names used in place of only initials in a reference? Would the source consequently be more difficult to find? Regardless of the answers to these questions, universities are unyielding when it comes to students following citation and referencing standards, so there is no need to ponder the questions; you must follow strictly the standard you, your chair, or the university chose. Knowing the standard well before you begin your dissertation not only saves time, but makes long interruptions during writing less frequent, leading to better writing. Olivia found that learning a standard while trying to use it causes problems with writing:

> I thought that since the citation and referencing standard required for my dissertation was so well-documented that it would be easy to implement

while writing. Since I used many types of sources in my dissertation, I constantly had to refer to the book that contained the formatting requirements. I often spent several minutes formatting a citation and/or reference, and then had to reorient myself to what I was writing about to maintain writing continuity. At one point, I realized that I needed to memorize the formats of at least the citations so that I could move more quickly between citing and writing. I made a cheat sheet for each of the major citation types, and I shortly found myself referring to it less and less until I finally knew them. I wasted a lot of time referring to the book on how to format citations and references, but the other problem was returning to writing after each lookup.

Emma's experiences were a little different:

I admit that I am not a details person, and I do not do well with tedious tasks. It was therefore unsurprising to me that I had botched the formatting of the references in my dissertation. I thought I saw patterns where none existed, and as someone who hates tedious tasks, I always looked for shortcuts when formatting my references. For example, I noticed that most references contained an un-italicized part and an italicized part. I mistakenly assumed that the un-italicized part always appeared first, so I began making book titles un-italicized and italicizing the publisher's name. My chair pointed out my mistake and I ended up having to reformat all of my references. I hired an editor to double-check my work, and she found many mistakes that remained even after my edits. I recommend that all doctoral students either learn to format references before starting the dissertation, or get someone else to do it for them, especially if tedious work is not their strong point.

Citations and references are crucial to all dissertations; they form the basis for the justification of the study, provide evidence of a contribution to the literature, and help a student avoid plagiarism, among other functions. Since most universities force students to follow a citation and referencing standard strictly, familiarity with the standard allows a student to avoid seemingly unending interruptions while writing, a time when concentration is paramount to exposition of a topic. If you are not a details-oriented person, you will struggle with the formatting of citations and references, and should therefore plan to get external help with them.

32
Anything You Can Do

It is no secret that dissertations are difficult to write. Even people unfamiliar with doctoral programs and research use the dissertation as a metaphor for anything that is difficult to do, especially when it comes to writing (e.g., "I am not asking you to write a dissertation, I just need a few paragraphs outlining your plan"). To most students, the dissertation represents the most significant work they've created in their lives, and the most writing they've ever engaged in at one time. Dissertations require constant rethinking of content and exposition by both student and chair. They are long-term projects that take more than a few twists and turns before they are completed, and the result is usually unexpected when viewed as a whole.

The nature of dissertations is that they are written, revisited, revised, rewritten, and sometimes abandoned, the result of which is a fragmented document that contains redundancies, verbiage, errors, and misapplications, and that often deviates from the hallmarks of scholarly writing. Some parts are written once, while others are rewritten multiple times, often months apart, and author fatigue and disparity of content exacerbate the fragmentation. Most of the students I've spoken to admit that their writing improved over time, making early writing distinguishable from later writing, again adding to discontinuity. You should then find it unsurprising that as a copyeditor, I recommend that the final version of every dissertation be copyedited professionally to remove errors, make the text generally more scholarly, and give the dissertation a single voice. Carlton found out the hard way that money spent on copyediting is far cheaper than an extended program:

> My chair and committee had officially approved my dissertation with the stipulation that the text get copyedited before submission to the graduate school for approval. I mistakenly assumed that my wife and I could

both read through the dissertation casually and fix any errors. When I submitted the dissertation to the graduate office, I found out that the university had strict rules regarding how the text should appear, and if the dissertation went beyond two inspections, the university began charging hefty fees for subsequent inspections. I also ran out of time to graduate in the current semester and had to register for another semester to remain matriculated. I eventually had the dissertation copyedited by a professional, and the amount charged was a pittance in comparison to the inspection fees and having to register for an additional semester.

Marcus's experience was similar:

I rewrote my dissertation so many times that no part seemed to match any other. When I neared the end of the dissertation, my chair recommended copyediting, and even "suggested" (required) hiring a specific copyeditor. I begrudgingly hired the copyeditor, but was later pleasantly surprised by how well the dissertation read after the edit. I have since hired that same copyeditor multiple times to make my writing better, and I believe that it is money well spent. The best part is that I benefitted from copyediting twice—once when I submitted the dissertation to my committee for approval, and again when I published parts of the dissertation in academic journals.

Experienced writers know that editing your own work is like performing brain surgery on yourself. When it comes to their own writing, authors see what they think they have written, not what really appears in the document. The inevitable fragmentation of a lengthy manuscript such as a dissertation, and the nascence most students have with scholarly writing, combine to create a document that is verbose and pedantic, and consequently fatiguing to read. The last thing you want to do is put your chair and committee to sleep while they read your dissertation. If you think your dissertation might benefit from copyediting, it will. Think of copyediting as an investment that returns dividends to you more than once. The cost up front might be unpleasant, especially since most doctoral students are running low on money by the end of their programs, but you get to benefit from the copyedit more than once. If you anticipate the expense long in advance, the costs will be offset by your smart planning.

33
Experience Trumps Logic

Suppose you needed to build a house to complete your doctoral program, but you have never seen a house in your life. Would it make sense to start buying supplies, such as concrete, wood, plaster, etc., without first knowing what materials you needed and how much of each material to buy, not to mention a plan to use those materials to construct the house? As strange as it may seem, many doctoral students begin their dissertations without any idea of what a dissertation looks like, especially regarding what the university and chair consider to be a satisfactory dissertation.

Some students view the dissertation as a journey, but even a journey taken casually must include some type of plan regarding where the traveler is going, how he/she will get there, and what he/she will see after arriving at the destination. Haphazardly planned journeys might be exciting to take, but that is no way to embark on a dissertation. Before beginning your own dissertation, you should examine products of former students' dissertations so you can get a feel for what is expected of you. The more you read, the better, but remember that not all dissertations will pertain directly to the topic you expose with your own dissertation. As an instrument of knowledge creation, each dissertation is unique and can serve only as a guide to dissertations that follow. Aiden proceeded with his dissertation without a clear idea of what was expected of him, and his progress suffered as a result:

> I began writing the proposal for my dissertation without a clear idea of what the dissertation would or should look like when it was done. I thought it would somehow progress naturally, and that it would take the correct shape eventually. My chair rejected much of what I submitted for the proposal, and there were many revisions, redirections, and rewrites. After several grueling months, I sought help from a dissertation coach, who asked me, "What will your dissertation look like when it is finished?" I struggled with the answer, so my coach had me look at dissertations

similar to my own so I could get an idea of what mine would look like when completed. This exercise stuck with me throughout the dissertation because I could not believe that I started something without any idea of how it would end up.

Ava's experiences were more serious:

When I started thinking about the proposal to my dissertation, I looked to dissertations completed by former students of my university to get an idea of what a dissertation was. I admit that I was clueless on this topic. However, I made the mistake of reading those dissertations for the topic they covered, not for how the topic was discussed. I gained a clear idea of what topics are appropriate for a dissertation, but I failed to notice how the topics were exposed. As my copyeditor later informed me, I read for content, not structure or style. With my copyeditor's help, I was able to remove the judgmental tone and redundancies that dominated my dissertation to create one that emulated those I had read months earlier. My advice to doctoral students at the dissertation stage of their programs is to read past dissertations twice—once for content and once for exposition. It takes longer, but it is well worth knowing what you are getting into before you begin.

Ideal dissertations to read before you begin your own are those 1) written by recent graduates of your university, 2) within the same scope or field as your program, and 3) written by your chair's former students. When you read those dissertations, remember that you are not reading them for content. Notice the way that those authors formed their arguments, and try to discover the gap that those authors filled with their studies. Were the gaps easy to find, or did you have to dig into the dissertation to find them? When you answer these questions, ask them of your own dissertation and try to imagine what yours will look like when it is completed. Until you can imagine the product of your dissertation, you will be lost in the forest without a compass.

34
Now and Later

Consult any book or expert on the topic of completing long-term, complex projects and you will be told to break a project into pieces to make it manageable, and so you can set goals to give yourself a sense of accomplishment along the way. Unfortunately, that advice is flawed in isolation because it is too easy to get embroiled in the details, ignore the big picture, and lose sight of what the finished product is supposed to look like and do. In essence, proceeding linearly through a long-term, complex project means that the pieces might not fit together during later stages.

A dissertation is certainly a long-term, complex project, but the problem with dissertations is that they come automatically broken up into pieces, such as the proposal, the individual chapters, the defense, etc., making a linear approach appear natural. Intuitive as it might be to tackle these pieces one at a time, doctoral students commonly find that they, for example, made promises in the proposal that they couldn't keep, or assumed that the dissertation's design should be dealt with only while writing the methods chapter. Dissertations are so long and complex that they appear to comprise smaller projects, especially when it comes to their chapters. However, thinking of a dissertation's chapters as smaller projects makes the larger project, the entire dissertation, much more difficult to imagine. Liam discovered this misperception about halfway through his dissertation:

> I submitted my dissertation chapter by chapter as required, but when I got to the methods chapter, I realized that the method I had chosen, and the one that was approved in my proposal, was incapable of testing the hypotheses I developed for the dissertation. I tried for a few weeks, which turned into months, to make the original methods work, but in the end, I had to admit to my chair that I needed to change methods to proceed with the study. The process was difficult, requiring many jumps through many hoops, and some cutting of red tape. I had to discuss the issue and

my solution with my chair and each of the committee members, which was difficult because they were all busy and hard to track down. I had to hold a second miniature proposal defense to update the chair and committee of the changes required to proceed with the dissertation. It worked out, but I should have planned the entire dissertation better.

Charlotte found that linear completion of a dissertation creates problems down the road:

I struggled to get my dissertation's proposal approved, but lack of foresight almost led to having to scrap the entire proposal and begin again. My proposal called for me to collect data using many validated instruments. Unfortunately, I did not calculate the number of items needed to collect all of the data, and the survey ended up with over 200 items that the participants in the study needed to complete. This was far too many and far too time-consuming, but the real problem had to do with the fatigue that the participants would experience while completing the survey, which would likely affect the results. I spent about two months searching for alternative, shorter instruments, and I eventually got the number of items on the survey down to about 90. Since altering the model that I was testing was impossible, given the purpose of the study, reducing the survey's length was my only choice. I should have paid more attention to the whole dissertation instead of working on it one step at a time.

Balancing detail and global perspectives of a dissertation is essential to ensuring that the pieces fit together when the dissertation is complete. Every once in a while, it makes sense to step back from the dissertation and see if there are any global roadblocks that can't be seen while working on one of the dissertation's details. Although you might be required to submit a dissertation chapter by chapter, a dissertation should not be planned that way. Switching between detail and global perspectives of a long-term, complex project is a skill. If you find it difficult to do, schedule regular times to consider global aspects of the dissertation until it becomes second nature to you.

35
A Hand to Hold

Most people involved in doctoral education—professors, students, administrators—spend little time thinking or discussing how education works because everyone presumably already knows how it works. Teachers teach, students learn, and the process repeats and evolves. However, some aspects of doctoral education are not a part of lower levels. The transition that students make from student to independent researcher during the dissertation is a journey taken alone, with occasional insights and advice from a chair who is there partially to guide and partially to observe. It often takes doctoral students a while to adjust to the change.

Like the other levels of higher education, doctoral programs begin with formal classroom lectures, seminars, and graded assignments, reinforcing traditional instructor–student relationships. However, as students move beyond coursework, a period characterized by teaching experiences, research assisting, practicums, comprehensive examinations, and other aspects of doctoral education that prepare students for their careers, relationships between professors and students diminish from one of teaching and judging to one of judging alone. For most doctoral students, this is a time of confusion because they realize that past education models no longer apply. They are on their own to demonstrate that they are making the transition from student to researcher, but the need for affirmation and guidance from a superior lingers. Nowhere is this felt more strongly than during development of a dissertation's proposal, when the student is struggling for the first time to simultaneously make that transition and still gain approval from the chair. Chloe's experiences exemplify this struggle:

> After my comprehensive examinations, I enrolled in the university's pre-dissertation course and waited for my chair to contact me to begin the proposal stage of the dissertation. After about three weeks, I was getting

nervous because time was slipping away and I was anxious to get started. I finally contacted my chair and we set up a meeting. At the meeting, my chair asked me about the progress I had made on the proposal, and since I had made none, I stammered on about a few ideas I had. I was surprised at how little help my chair was providing. I was expecting at least a brief lecture on how we would proceed, or at least a discussion of milestones and scheduling. Instead, I was facing a totally different person from the one I had known during my coursework. He wasn't cold or disinterested, he just didn't provide me with the help I was initially expecting.

Ryan's experiences were similar:

When I began writing the proposal for my dissertation, my chair asked me for regular updates (e.g., weekly, semi-monthly, etc.) so that he could keep apprised of my progress. I would send him an e-mail weekly, but he never responded, so I just kept going. I assumed that at some point he would catch up with me about the progress I was making. When I hit what I thought was the mid-point of the proposal, I thought it prudent to stop by my chair's office to see why he had not responded. He thanked me for the e-mailed updates and asked when I thought I would have the proposal ready for his inspection. I said I was about half done, and that I would have the proposal ready in about another 6 weeks. He was pleased and said he looked forward to seeing it. It was then that I learned that the feedback I was expecting was not going to come. I was on my own to write the proposal. I did not waste any time because I never stopped working, but I spent a few nerve-racking weeks waiting for input that was never to come.

Doctoral students draw from past education to make assumptions about how the proposal stage will proceed. Most are surprised by the dearth of guidance they receive, but this experience varies from chair to chair. It is wise to assume that your chair is playing the role of observer rather than guide until you get a better sense of what role your chair plans to play in your dissertation. The safest approach is to assume that you can assume nothing, and use current experiences to characterize the relationship your chair will have with you.

36
Research What You Know

The aphorism *write what you know* applies equally to research, in the form *research what you know*. This advice is not intended to limit authors, but to make writing easier, and make it engaging for the reader. As a copyeditor, it is always obvious to me when an author was uncomfortable writing about a topic, and with all of the other challenges that accompany completing a dissertation, writing about an unknown topic amplifies the difficulty. It is therefore surprising that some doctoral students choose topics outside of their expertise, often motivated by the difficulty of finding a topic to pursue.

Speaking of aphorisms, one you've probably heard is *the best dissertation is a signed dissertation*. There will be plenty of time during your career to pursue any research topics you desire. However, for the dissertation, conservatism goes a long way. Ask yourself, "Why did I spend the past several years becoming an expert in a field only to deviate from that field to pursue another during my dissertation?" The dissertation already involves much learning. Why add to that learning by pursuing an unfamiliar topic, and thereby increase the chances that you will abandon the dissertation or be unable to finish it? The problem starts early during the proposal stage, a time when doctoral students struggle to find a topic to pursue or gap to fill. Most doctoral students have trouble discovering a gap in the literature to address with a dissertation, and therefore hold on to one they think they found even if that gap appears in other, albeit related, literature. Ethan learned that choosing a topic outside of his expertise wastes a lot of time:

I found a topic to explore in my dissertation early during my program. I thought that since no research had been conducted on the topic in my field that I had found a vital research gap that I could fill. The topic had been covered in other fields, but ones that used theories, models, and perspectives unfamiliar to me. I spent months learning them so that I could approach the topic, but I found myself mired in complications that seemed to unfold continuously. I realize now that I should have been less rigid regarding the topic I chose for the dissertation, and I should not have chosen a topic so early during my studies. My advice to doctoral students is to be open-minded about the topic of your dissertation. The most important thing is getting the dissertation done.

Zhang put himself in a similar situation:

My program focused on qualitative designs, and to the best of my knowledge, all previous doctoral students in my program used qualitative methods. However, I initially chose a quantitative design for my dissertation. I had never been trained to use quantitative methods, and I made some wild assumptions about what was involved. Issues such as validity, single-source bias, and sampling were unknown to me, but I powered through and submitted a proposal that included quantitative methods. One of my committee members was a quantitative researcher, and she clued me in to the mistakes I was making and what it would take to fix them. After three months of struggling, I gave up and moved to a qualitative design. Although I am still interested in using quantitative methods, I should have stuck with what I knew and was trained to do for the dissertation, and moved to quantitative designs later.

Dissertations are difficult enough without adding more to do, and worry about, while engaged in one. Although it is common for dissertations to require learning on the part of the researcher to complete, delving outside of an area of expertise adds another front to the battle because it involves unguided learning; the student must self-learn doctoral-level topics to proceed. Researching what you know is the surest way to develop a proposal and conduct the study associated with a dissertation to completion with the fewest errors, roadblocks, and rewrites. When you think you found a topic for your dissertation to focus on, ask yourself whether it lies too far outside of your expertise. If so, keep looking, or find a way to bring the topic into your area of expertise using what you already know.

37
Yellow Research

Students do not choose a field to pursue at the doctoral level randomly; they are motivated by personal interest and their learning experiences at other levels of education, especially what they learned at the Master's level, and even experiences at work. Such personal interests can get in the way of completing a dissertation because the researcher is too close to or too passionate about a topic. The result is a dissertation that is abandoned or needs to be rewritten to conform to scholarly standards, regardless of the methods used to expose a topic. In either case, this means a longer program and consequently reduced likelihood of completion.

In all aspects of life, passion for a field, topic, profession, hobby, etc. increases the chances that progress is made; it is a motivational force that reduces procrastination and increases perceptions of efficacy. Having passion for a topic pursued in a dissertation sounds like a positive attribute to have, one that makes working on a dissertation seem less like work and more like a choice, and it is. However, passion for a topic also makes researchers deviate from objectivity, pursue topics for personal or political reasons, and violate precepts of scientific discovery, even when subjectivity is part of a study's design. Students who do this are lulled into thinking that they are making great progress on a dissertation, only to find later that their chairs and committee members require major rewrites so that the dissertation represents balanced views or conforms more rigorously to the methods chosen for the dissertation. Benjamin had to restructure several chapters of his dissertation to reduce personal bias:

> The qualitative design I chose for my dissertation required me to engage participants in deep dialogues about a problem they were facing. I spent many months interacting with them, gaining knowledge about the antecedents of their dilemma. This part of the dissertation was acceptable to

my chair, but she felt that previous chapters contained biased language, suggesting that my interest and investment in the participants made it impossible for me to find fault with them. I truly wanted to help them, but I had become so close to them that my sympathies got in the way of seeing what was really happening. I was able to rewrite earlier chapters to my chair's satisfaction, but I can now see how compassion for people clouds objectivity in research.

Emily's history with the subjects of her dissertation similarly clouded her objectivity:

I worked as a social worker for many years with a group of people whose children had a high dropout rate from high school. I chose this problem as the topic of my dissertation, and my design required that I interview parents to assess whether there was a common cause across families. When I showed the interview questions to my chair, he noticed that they focused only on external causes of the problem, making it impossible to discover causes related to families. My dissertation would therefore exclude the possibility that the parents were at least partially at fault for the high dropout rate, a finding I did not wish to reveal due to my closeness with the participants. My chair and I worked closely to develop interview questions that explored a range of causes, not just the ones I wanted to find. My advice to doctoral students is to remember that even designs that use subjectivity to expose a topic require that all possible causes of a problem be explored, not just the ones that are interesting to you or ones that you believe are the cause.

Objectivity in research is not solely the domain of better designs, validated instruments, and peer reviews. Some designs require subjectivity to expose a topic, but even within that subjectivity, researchers need to ensure that they are not guiding results to a conclusion they desire. Passion for a topic is a powerful motivator that can also impede good scientific research and discoveries. Be careful of the designs and subjects you choose for your dissertation. You might be too close or too passionate about a topic to be objective, and you might end up hurting the very people you intended to help by ignoring an important cause or factor related to their problem.

38
Sunk Costs

Investment of any kind—money, time, effort—should return at least a modicum of benefit to the investor in exchange for the expenditure, but life is too complicated and unpredictable to expect all investments to pay off. One business precept suggests that there is no point to chasing bad money with good money; once an investment will not or cannot return a positive outcome, there is no reason to invest more in the same investment in hopes that the situation will reverse. Such investments represent sunk costs because they are already lost and cannot be recovered. Unfortunately, vanity and an unwillingness to accept a loss make some investors spend more chasing a futile investment. The concept of sunk costs applies to dissertations.

Dissertations inevitably lead all doctoral students to dead ends, missed opportunities, wasted time, and even lost money. Recognizing when a course of action will not return a positive outcome is essential to making the dissertation take as little time as possible to complete. The longer a dissertation takes to complete, the more likely it will not be completed, and consequently, pursuing dead investments, or sunk costs, is detrimental to a doctoral student's completion of a program. Sometimes you just have to let some ideas go to progress with the dissertation, but doing so can be psychologically difficult when so much was invested in them. Needing to overcome the desire to chase a sunk cost is something all doctoral students experience during a dissertation. Carter learned the hard way that sunk costs should not be chased:

> While trying to find a gap in the literature that my dissertation could address, I found a study that suggested that a variable used across many studies in my field did not correlate with another dependent variable. I built my entire proposal around this finding, thinking that I would explore

the topic and put the debate to rest. My chair was against the idea because although this one study suggested no correlation, there were many more that suggested the opposite. I returned to my chair week after week to try to convince her that the study was worth pursuing, but she said no each time. I finally gave up and moved on to another topic. I realize now that it was irrational to waste so much time trying to convince my chair that I should study something that she had already rejected several times.

Jayden's relentlessness almost cost him his degree:

I collected a lot of data for my dissertation and all was going well until I tested my hypotheses and found that only 1 of 8 were supported. I relayed this information to my chair, who told me that I would have to redevelop the hypotheses and collect new data until a satisfactory number of them were supported. I was disappointed, and I spent the next few weeks arguing with my chair that my non-significant results still represented a contribution to the literature. I even wrote a draft of the discussion chapter to show that I could turn my findings into an important contribution. He disagreed with me every step of the way, but I persisted because I did not want to have wasted so much time collecting and analyzing the data, and the prospect of doing it all again to uncertain results was unappealing. Eventually, my chair refused to consider the findings, forcing me to move forward with his suggestion.

Chasing sunk costs only leads to greater losses, but people assume that investments must eventually pay out, so they allow their desires to cloud good judgement. Finding a gap to fill in the literature is a difficult process, and so some students become relentless in trying to make a gap that they think they found pay out in the form of the chair's approval. Undesirable results represent another area in which students are relentless to realize a positive payout. Research is an investment in time, effort, and money, and like all investments, research represents risk. Learn to recognize sunk costs so you can move on to productive behaviors that get you closer to a completed dissertation. If you can't, you are working under a handicap that might derail your program.

39
But I Never Learned That

Everyone, including your chair, understands that you cannot work on your dissertation 24 hours each day and 365 days each year. You need to take breaks to recharge yourself, gain fresh perspectives on the dissertation's content, and attend to other areas of your life. However, as a dissertation coach, I have noticed a trend among doctoral students when they encounter a roadblock to completing the dissertation—they avoid the dissertation for long periods rather than face obstacles.

Dissertations are complex, multifaceted projects that take a long time to complete and force students to learn while doing; they are rarely only demonstrations of ability. Consequently, doctoral students run into tasks, especially regarding research design and data analysis, that are beyond their capability, requiring them to learn something new before being able to continue. When doctoral students run into these roadblocks, they do one of two things. They either retreat, which involves avoiding the roadblock by engaging in busy work such as reorganizing references, recreating tables, redesigning figures, etc., or they advance, facing the problem by learning what they need to know and moving forward with the dissertation. Retreating often leads to long-term avoidance of the dissertation, and is an early symptom of dissertation abandonment, which ultimately leads to a student failing to finish the dissertation and consequently the program. Advancement, the more difficult of the two choices, is often met with resentment and anger because many doctoral students misperceive that the dissertation is, or should be, simply a demonstration of things learned past. Tara's experiences offer an important lesson:

> My proposal called for using linear regression to test a series of hypotheses that I constructed into a model that explained cognitions and the behaviors that resulted from them. Throughout the entire dissertation, my

chair and I discussed that I would test the hypotheses using linear regression. I was relieved because I was unfamiliar with other methods, and statistics was never a strong subject for me. Just before I started analyzing the data, one of my committee members casually commented that I should switch to structural equation modeling since I was assessing latent variables. My chair and the remaining members of the committee agreed, and I was left to self-learn how to conduct analyses using the method. I assumed that learning structural equation modeling would be difficult, so I avoided it by attending to other dissertation tasks. I also resented the switch that my chair and committee forced me to make since structural equation modeling was not part of my program. About two months later, I realized that I couldn't put it off any longer. So, I read some books and searched on the Internet for lessons on the topic, and I also consulted with a few statistics experts. In the end, I learned that the technique was not too complicated, and I was able to complete the analyses and interpret the results without too much trouble. I realize now that the switch to structural equation modeling made sense given the type of data I had, but I wish I had not brooded about it, delaying the completion of the dissertation.

Sean's story is similar:

My doctoral program trained me to be a quantitative researcher. All of the methods and statistics courses that the program required reinforced the fact that my dissertation would use a quantitative design. I was therefore flabbergasted when my chair told me that I needed to use a qualitative design to answer the research questions I developed for my proposal. None of the doctoral courses I took focused on qualitative research, and some of my past professors, none of whom were members of my committee, talked pejoratively about qualitative designs, even though it was usually in jest. I spent the next three months avoiding learning about qualitative designs because I thought it was unfair that I should have to use something that I didn't learn earlier in the program.

If you are like most doctoral students, your dissertation will require you to learn something new. Transitioning from student to researcher is a demonstration of independence, not knowledge alone. You need to demonstrate that you can overcome obstacles and act independently, and your chair is there to observe that you do.

40
Even Steven

Teachers, college professors included, strive for pedagogies that are equitable among students; all students receive the same instruction, take the same tests, and are graded the same way to ensure fairness. However, fairness cannot be guaranteed because some aspects that affect learning, including a student's knowledge, motivation, and home life, are out of a teacher's control. At best, the system is fair, even if each student's experiences in it are not. Disparities among students appear even at the doctoral level because doctoral students vary when it comes to ability, motivation, and extra-university challenges (e.g., children, family, work, etc.). The result is a unique doctoral experience for each student.

Most doctoral programs, either formally or informally, group doctoral students into cohorts according to the time or year they were admitted to the program. Students in a cohort typically take the same classes together and progress through the first couple of years at the same pace. Some even take comprehensive examinations at the same time. However, members of a cohort typically cease to progress equally once they begin working on their dissertation proposals. It is common for some doctoral students to finish their proposals months and sometimes even years ahead of other members of the cohort because each dissertation is a unique contribution to the literature, and variations in topics, approaches, methods, and outcomes lengthen or shorten the time it takes to complete a study. Add to that the variations among students in terms of abilities, motivations, and time available to work on the dissertation, and it is easy to see why some students finish a doctoral program long before others who started at the same time. Riley felt left behind when other members of her cohort were progressing quicker than she was:

Several students were accepted into the doctoral program at the same time I was, and we moved through the program at nearly the same pace for about three years. This all changed when we began creating our proposals for our dissertations. We all had different chairs, and it seemed that some students were having an easier time convincing their chairs that their proposals were filling a significant gap in the literature to proceed with the dissertation. At about 6 months after we began our proposals, 3 of 5 of us had already defended their proposals and a 4th was about to do so. I was so far behind that I thought perhaps that my chair was sending me a message about my ability to complete the program. I finally defended my proposal about 8 months after everyone else in my group, and I graduated about one year after everyone. For some reason, I thought we would all progress more or less at the same pace.

Zoe nearly quit her program because she thought she was too far behind:

All of the members of my cohort were ahead of me when it came to defending the proposal, so I was elated when my proposal defense was finally scheduled. You can imagine my disappointment when I failed to convince my committee that my dissertation should proceed, and I needed to go back to the drawing board regarding several aspects of my proposal. I seriously considered quitting the program because I was embarrassed to be so far behind the others. However, I stuck with it, and once my proposal was defended, I proceeded with the dissertation and even graduated a few months ahead of those who were ahead of me.

Every study—dissertations included—represent unique contributions to a field. They cannot be compared in terms of how long it takes to conduct them. Some minor studies take years to complete and some high-influence ones can be completed in a matter of months. Dissertations typically take longer because they are being conducted by nascent researchers. How long it takes to conduct a study is never an indication of its influence on the literature or the competency of the researcher. Don't compare your progress with the proposal, or any stage of the dissertation, by comparing your progress with that of your cohorts. Perseverance is the greatest predictor of finishing a dissertation, not the speed by which it is completed in comparison to others.

41
Relative Proportioning

Dissertation proposals take several forms across universities, departments, and chairs, but the most common are the first three chapters of the dissertation, or a prospectus, which is an outline of the topics and methods that the dissertation will address and use. Even in the case of the former, most proposals are shorter than what appears in the completed dissertation, and it is common for proposals to be shorter than 75 pages, including citations, references, and supplemental material. The brevity of a dissertation's proposal often creates a perceptual error that gets many doctoral students into trouble, causing endless revisions that can take months or longer to correct, and even fatal errors.

Think of the dissertation proposal as a plan—a schedule and course of action rolled into one that guides the dissertation to completion. A dissertation is a major undertaking, so it makes sense to create a sound plan that will increase your chances of finishing it. Unfortunately, many students view the proposal—the plan—as less important than the dissertation itself, and therefore proportion time spent creating the proposal in relation to the dissertation's length. In other words, since the proposal is shorter than the dissertation, students spend less time on it, assuming that length represents importance, and anything inexplicit in the proposal will be figured out later when the real work begins. However, during most major undertakings, planning takes longer than execution. Treating the proposal as less important than the dissertation means that many students run into roadblocks and even face fatal errors later because their plans were either flawed or incomplete. Harper took her dissertation's proposal less seriously than she should have:

> The proposal for my dissertation was a prospectus that outlined the major aspects of the study I was conducting. I knew what I wanted to study, but

my skills with methods and analysis were lacking at the time, and I didn't put much effort into explaining them in the prospectus because I knew I had some learning to do on those topics. My chair would not accept my first prospectus because I was too vague with topics I was uncomfortable with, leading me to go through many rounds of submission and revision until it was finally approved. Later during the dissertation, the prospectus became my best friend because it kept me on track, and I felt like I was simply executing a well-laid plan. My dissertation was not easy, but I can see how much harder it would have been if I started it with a half-baked plan. Time spent during the proposal stage pays large dividends later.

Isabella proportioned time spent on her proposal in relation to the length of the dissertation, and she experienced trouble later:

My chair required me to create what she called a mockup of the first three chapters of my dissertation, which then represented my proposal. The mockup was less detailed than the dissertation would be, but it needed to include all of the major elements, arguments, and methods that would eventually become part of the dissertation. I saw the proposal as a shell or framework on which the dissertation would be built, but I didn't realize that the framework I had created was missing details that couldn't be fixed later. I chose a design that could not answer my research questions because I did not consider how I would actually use the data once I had them. I realize now that I should have planned my dissertation more carefully, instead of assuming that it would evolve in the direction I needed it to.

While planning any activity, it makes sense to spend the most time on parts that either return the most benefit or have the potential to create the greatest loss. Dissertation proposals represent a plan that you must execute, and the more time spent agonizing over the benefits and losses you will likely encounter along the way, the smoother the dissertation is likely to proceed. Although the proposal might seem like a project itself, it is really a roadmap to dissertation success. Don't be tempted to determine the time to spend on a proposal by considering its length in relation to the length of the dissertation.

42
Novice Expert

A wise professor once told me that if I wanted to learn to teach well, I first needed to be a true expert on the topic, and nothing demonstrates expertise better than being able to discuss all aspects of a topic off the top of your head. Dissertation proposals often go through numerous revisions, restructures, and rewrites, so it is common for students to get confused about what the final proposal contains. That process is an important part of learning to create a study, and many chairs organize it that way to show the student that research can be a complicated business, and dealing with those complications is part of the transition to independent researcher.

While I was a dissertation coach, many students came to me after their proposal defenses seeking help with getting started with their dissertations. During initial meetings, I asked students to tell me about their studies, but few students could tell me off the top of their heads what their studies were doing. I could hear papers rustling and computer keyboards clicking in the background as the students looked for answers. This was especially surprising since the students' proposal defenses were only a few days or weeks prior to our conversations. I didn't expect the students to have memorized every detail of the study, but I did expect a one-liner that explained what variables were being tested, in what contexts, and with what methods. Being an expert on your own dissertation means that you hold firmly in your head what you are doing and why, making every aspect of the dissertation, especially writing its chapters, easier because you always know what you are doing and therefore won't stray off topic, something that is easy to do during a project measured in months or years. Ethan found that being unclear about the basics of his proposal made his dissertation difficult to write:

My chair often complained that I was getting too far off topic with my dissertation. I would rewrite sections but my chair still insisted that they either be revised or removed. I sought help from an expert in my field, and he asked me what my dissertation was about. I said I would send him my proposal, but he wanted to hear about it directly from me. I found it difficult to articulate what my dissertation was accomplishing, and he told me that that was the problem. He asked me to summarize the entire dissertation proposal using only one sentence, which should then serve as my dissertation's mission statement. He even suggested that I print the sentence on paper and tape it to my monitor so that when I was writing, I could look up at it occasionally and ask whether what I was writing, or about to write, contributed to that mission statement. The trick worked and my focus improved, with the result of fewer rejections from my chair.

Logan's experience hit his ego hard:

I was having trouble with a validated instrument that I was using in my dissertation concerning how to calculate scores from the items. I called the researcher who developed it, and he asked me for a summary of my dissertation. I went blank because my dissertation had deviated from the proposal slightly, though the main study was largely intact. I was embarrassed that I had to put the professor on hold while I looked for a copy of my proposal to read from. The experience had no effect on my program, but I knew that I needed to get what I was doing with my dissertation straight before I embarrassed myself in front of my chair or committee.

Nothing demonstrates nascence more than unfamiliarity with a topic. No one is more of an expert on your dissertation's proposal than you are, and you cannot demonstrate your expertise unless you can discuss your proposal with confidence. Your chair and committee members are constantly judging you. Ensure that you can talk intelligently and confidently about your dissertation with anyone who asks about it. Doing so will keep your dissertation on track, help with writing, and project an image of confidence, ability, and expertise to the people judging your dissertation, and you as a researcher.

43
Quick Lunch

During education prior to your doctoral program, you learned and were tested on that learning through a variety of means, such as written tests, oral exams, papers, and presentations. However, none of those tests were a formality; they were designed to create variation in the scoring among students in a class so that a clear demarcation was made among those who excelled, those who performed averagely, and those who failed to meet minimum standards. Your grade was based on your performance on these tests, and although your instructors helped you to do well on them, it was not guaranteed that you would.

Developing a dissertation proposal is the responsibility of the student, but there are other people, or stakeholders, involved, including the chair, committee members, the department, the university, etc. Just like the instructors who taught you during previous programs, the people involved in your dissertation provide various types of help when you are developing your dissertation proposal, and just like the tests that gauged your learning in previous programs, the proposal defense is not a formality. It is a test that demonstrates your readiness to proceed with your dissertation, and some students pass and are authorized to begin the dissertation, and some students fail and must revise the proposal until it meets minimum standards. Too many doctoral students think that the proposal defense's outcome is set in stone before the defense takes place, making many students complacent about doing well during the defense. Adalyn thought that the defense was a formality, and was shocked when she learned that it wasn't:

The time and effort I invested in creating the proposal for my dissertation was considerable since I needed to make many revisions at the insistence of my chair and committee. So, I was especially relieved when my chair told me that it was time for the defense. I figured that the time and effort that went into the proposal meant that I was ready to move on to the dissertation itself, and that the defense was the formal declaration of moving to the next stage. At the defense, I was met with a barrage of questions and doubtful comments regarding whether my study was viable, and whether I could complete it. The most surprising part was that even my chair was doubtful about some areas of my proposal. I assumed that the defense would go smoothly since the people who helped me develop it were also the people judging it. I could not understand why they would let me defend if they had reservations about what I was proposing.

Aaliyah also expected the proposal defense to be a formality:

When the defense for my dissertation's proposal was scheduled, I thought that I would do well since my chair was the one who decided that the proposal was ready for defense. During the defense, several committee members expressed concerns about whether I would be able to conduct the study. Much of the objection revolved around whether I had sufficient knowledge of the design I had chosen. I admit that I had little knowledge of the design, but it was the most common one the literature uses when studying the topic that I chose for my dissertation. My chair and committee asked me for a supplementary defense in a week's time, during which I would demonstrate that I understood the design of my study well enough to use it. I did well at the supplementary defense and was allowed to proceed with the dissertation, but I still thought it odd that the objections were not brought up before the defense.

The proposal defense is a test, though not solely of the study being proposed. Your chair and committee are also testing whether you are capable of transforming your proposal into the study you are proposing. There must be a match between the study and your ability to conduct it and see it through to completion. Consequently, the study might be sound, but your chair and committee might question whether you can conduct it. A proposal defense is typically scheduled once a study is viable, but the defense is not a formality; you must convince your chair and committee that you can do it.

44
Skipping Class

There is an old public speaker's trick: standing at the front of the empty room in which a near-future speech will be delivered has a calming effect on the speaker because he/she experiences fewer unfamiliar visual stimuli that can be distracting when the speech is given. In essence, familiarity makes us feel safe, and knowledge about an unknown increases efficacy. At all stages of the dissertation, witnessing what other people are experiencing helps a doctoral student reduce anxiety concerning the unknown, and nowhere is that advice more appropriate than when it comes to defending a proposal in front of a chair, committee members, and other attendees. I find that most students are more anxious about the proposal defense than the dissertation defense because everything is new, and it is the first oral defense in the dissertation process.

Proposal defenses usually follow a similar pattern—the student presents the proposal, attendees ask questions and make suggestions, to which the student responds, and the chair and committee members deliberate to arrive at a decision to approve or disapprove of the proposal. It sounds clinical and logical enough, but making assumptions at any stage of the dissertation is what gets students into trouble, even when they have to do with the process of the dissertation, not the dissertation itself. Any knowledge you can acquire along the way to your own proposal defense can only help you understand the process, so it is surprising that so few doctoral students attend other doctoral students' proposal defenses to see what they are all about. Alexander was stunned by the format of his proposal defense:

I created an elaborate electronic slide presentation for my proposal defense because I thought that the defense would take the form of a presentation. I thought that I would present the justification, methods, and expected findings of my dissertation, answer a few questions, and then leave the room while my committee discussed whether I would be allowed to proceed with the study. However, when I arrived at the room where the proposal defense was scheduled to take place, there was no projector to connect my laptop to, and there was no screen on which to display my electronic slide presentation. When my chair arrived, she informed me that the proposal would be a question-and-answer session, and I would have to answer my committee's questions without any aids. My chair told me later that there was no need for a formal presentation because all attendees had recently read my proposal, and there was no need for them to hear what they had just read. It turns out that all proposal defenses in my department went like this. I just didn't know because I never attended anyone else's proposal defense.

Caleb's proposal defense was also a surprise:

I attended a large, public university whose lecture halls held hundreds of people, so I was concerned when I learned at the last minute that my proposal defense was assigned to a large lecture hall. I thought perhaps that that was the only lecture hall available in that time slot, or that it was the only one that had the facilities needed for the defense. I thought I had walked into the wrong lecture hall when I saw that about half of the seats (about 100 people) were filled. I later learned that all proposal defenses on campus were open to the public. I assumed that the defense would be a more intimate affair between me and my committee. I was unprepared for that size of an audience, and it threw me off until I got used to it during my presentation.

Attending other doctoral students' proposal defenses is the best way to prepare for your own. You get a chance to see the format that your defense will use, and you can see where it will be held and who and how many people are likely to attend. If you can't attend a proposal defense, or if proposal defenses are closed at your university, ask doctoral students about their defenses to gain as much knowledge as you can about the defense's format, venue, and attendance. With that information, you can plan a better proposal defense and avoid unnecessary anxiety on the big day.

45
Entire of Itself

By the time doctoral students schedule the proposal defense, they are both exhausted and exhilarated by the process. They are exhausted because the journey was challenging, but are exhilarated that the dissertation is moving forward. However, the proposal defense still holds a few surprises that can derail even the most confident student, not because the student does not understand what the proposal says he/she will do during the dissertation, but because he/she is unprepared to address what won't be done during the dissertation. In essence, it is possible to know everything about your proposal and still do poorly during its defense.

Doctoral students assume that the proposal defense is a demonstration of knowledge of the proposal—what the student will study and how it will be studied. However, knowledge of the proposal itself is insufficient to excel during a defense. Planning to do anything includes a process of examining and excluding elements that were either inappropriate to the goal of the task or deemed insufficient to bring about a desired outcome. Dissertation proposals follow the same process. Doctoral students conducting empirical research, for example, must choose among quantitative and qualitative designs, sampling techniques, and statistics to answer research questions. In doing so, they determine not only what they will do, but also what they won't do. The proposal discusses only what a student will do, misrepresenting the process a student goes through to arrive at a viable study. Daniel discovered that knowledge of his proposal alone was insufficient during its defense:

> I did my best to memorize my proposal so that I could appear confident during the defense. My dissertation used a quantitative design that involved sampling subjects who worked in large corporations. While discussing my dissertation's design at the defense, one of my committee

members asked me to defend why I had chosen a quantitative design. I got through his questions well enough, until he asked me to describe what the study would look like if I had chosen a qualitative design, but I didn't know how to answer the question. I remember considering such issues while writing the proposal, but I was unprepared to discuss them at the defense. After the defense, my chair informed me that knowing what I was not going to do during the dissertation frames what I was going to do, and hence why it was brought up during the defense.

Jack experienced something similar during his proposal defense:

The attendees at the defense of my proposal remained largely quiet while I presented. I thought all was going well, and I gained confidence as I neared the end of the presentation that people were genuinely impressed with my proposal. However, one of the attendees, the outside reader of my dissertation, started asking questions about the results I expected, and what they would add to the literature. I didn't know how to answer because I had not yet gathered or analyzed the data, so I did not know what the results of the study would be, let alone what effect they would have on my field. He explained to me later that he wanted to get a sense of whether I understood the ramifications of my study, and whether I understood that the most important part of the study was its effect on the literature, not how well I had planned and presented the dissertation. He wanted to know as much about me as a researcher as he did about my study.

Memorizing the details of your proposal will make you appear confident and knowledgeable as a researcher, but what you propose to do to study your topic is framed by what you will not be doing. You might have chosen one method over another, but why? What makes the one you chose superior to the many alternatives available to you? Don't be surprised if the attendees at your defense ask questions that go beyond the document you gave to them to read in preparation for your defense. They are evaluating you as a researcher, in addition to judging the plans you laid out in your proposal. Be prepared to think beyond your plans; think like a researcher, not a student completing an assignment.

46
Orderly Affair

Dissertations are filled with surprises, occasionally unpleasant ones, and minimizing the unknown is essential to succeeding. If you've attended other doctoral students' proposal defenses, you have done all you can to minimize the unknowns about your own defense, though there is no way to perfectly predict future events from past events. Succeeding with the proposal defense requires the ability to adapt to any situation that might arise, and being an expert on your proposal, regarding both what you will and won't do with your dissertation, is essential to thriving on the chaos that might erupt during your defense.

Think back to the presentations you gave during your previous programs. Chances are you were given the floor to present your topic, and the presentation was an orderly affair; no one was allowed to interrupt you to ask a question or provide an opposing point of view. Dissertation proposal defenses do not always operate this way. It is common for attendees, especially chairs and committee members, to interject a comment or question, to which the student must respond on the spot. Some defenses are designed this way to pressure the student into demonstrating expertise with the proposal, the future dissertation, the topic, or the field as a whole. Some proposal defenses degenerate into arguments among attendees, and I know of a few cases when a defense had to be rescheduled because tempers flared too high. Admittedly, these represent extreme cases, but preparing for the worst means that you will be able to handle anything that arises during your defense. William experienced an extreme case during his proposal defense.

During my proposal defense, everything was going well until about halfway through when one of my committee members asked a question about the way I was collecting data. My chair tried to cut the committee member off before she could finish, but the committee member just kept

91

going. My chair became angry, insisting that this was not the time for questions about data collection. The committee member objected and a minor argument ensued. A few other members of my committee joined in on the argument, whose topic ranged from data collection to how the proposal defense should proceed. The incident lasted only about 4 or 5 minutes, but by the time I was allowed to continue, I was shaken by the behaviors of my chair and committee members. I stumbled through the remainder of the defense, unsure of how to deal with these events.

Avery's experiences demonstrate just how disorderly a proposal defense can be:

I planned my proposal defense carefully, assuming that the best approach was to discuss the chapters of my dissertation in order. I started with the introductory chapter, but then one of my committee members asked about who I intended to use as subjects for the study. To me, that was an issue for the methods chapter, and I was unprepared to skip ahead and then back. I did my best to answer the question, and then strategically moved my discussion back to the introductory chapter so I could continue. Unfortunately, I was interrupted so many times that I could not keep track of where I was in the presentation. I planned it carefully, and it made sense to me only if I walked my chair and committee members through the proposal one step at a time. By being forced to skip around, I could not keep track of what I had discussed and what was left to discuss. I assumed that I would be allowed to present the proposal uninterrupted, with perhaps an occasional clarifying question from my chair or a committee member here or there at worst.

As with most aspects of a dissertation, proposal defenses rarely go as the student expected. Remember that your chair and committee members have already read your proposal, so they don't need it reiterated to them orally. Chairs and committee members come to a defense prepared to bring up concerns and ask questions, and most students are surprised at how informal some proposal defenses can be. Don't assume that your proposal defense will be a formal or orderly affair. Very often, it is about the content of a proposal alone, not about how that content is presented.

47
Foregone Conclusion

Developing a dissertation proposal is a strange process. As if finding a gap in the literature, choosing a method that isolates variables and answers the research questions, and ensuring that the exposition of the dissertation contributes to a field were not enough, professors who once mentored the student through previous parts of the doctoral program suddenly appear aloof or unwilling to provide concrete guidance or encouragement on what seems like the most critical stage of the dissertation—the plan that will get the student through the program. This experience feels like abandonment, and often derails the student from making serious progress with the proposal.

The proposal defense is the culmination of developing a proposal; it is the point at which the student discovers whether he/she will be allowed to continue with the dissertation or must develop the proposal further. The chair and committee members decide when a proposal defense is warranted, and students breathe a sigh of relief when the proposal defense is scheduled because it both signals the completion of the proposal stage and represents a major milestone of the dissertation. However, the assumption that the proposal defense is synonymous with completion of development of a proposal is a misperception that makes students grow complacent. The assumption derives from the belief that since the people who decided that a student is ready for the proposal defense are also the people who will be judging the proposal, it is unthinkable that they would allow a student to defend unless acceptance were imminent. Students who had their proposals rejected during the proposal defense can tell you otherwise. Evelyn's rejected proposal surprised her immensely:

It took me nearly 6 months to get my chair to a point where she was ready to have me defend my proposal. I spoke with her and my committee members at length about what was expected of me during the defense, and some even coached me on how to present my proposal in the most flattering light. You can imagine my surprise when I "failed" my defense. Most of the concepts I intended to use during the dissertation were scrutinized heavily, and one committee member explicitly stated that my method was weak and suboptimal given the relationships I was testing. The thing most surprising to me was that these were the people who helped me develop these aspects of the proposal and showed me how to present them. I learned later that both the chair and committee members were there to help me make what I was proposing better, but would not suggest better approaches. I'm glad that I learned this lesson early because it served me well during the rest of the dissertation.

Arjun's defense outcome was also puzzling to him:

My chair made it clear to me that I would get only one chance to defend my proposal, with three possible outcomes: pass, in which case I would move on with the dissertation, fail, in which case I would need to retake a pre-dissertation course so I could either develop the proposal further or create a new one, and pass conditional, which means I would have one month to fix the proposal before informally demonstrating to my committee that the problems were fixed. My chair and committee members appeared confident about my proposal, so I thought that I would pass, or at least pass conditionally. Unfortunately, I failed the defense because I was unable to convince my chair and committee that the study needed to be added to the field's literature. To this day, I am unsure why they would allow me to defend if they intended to fail me.

Proposal defenses are not formalities or rites of passage. They represent the first time that a doctoral student is judged as an independent researcher, and the process and outcomes of a proposal defense can be ambiguous and confusing. Assuming that a committee will approve a proposal after it is defended is dangerous. However, learning that from now on you are being judged as an independent researcher, not a student, is a lesson better learned at the proposal stage than later. Be careful of the assumptions you make at all stages of the dissertation, and assume that you can assume nothing.

48
United They Stand

Whenever several people must agree on a topic, such as when an important decision must be made, there is likely to be disagreement on what should be done, how it should be done, and what resources should be used to realize a positive outcome. Conflicts regarding details, processes, and outcomes linger even after a decision is made, and tempers can resurface later when evaluating a decision and its outcomes. Deliberations among dissertation committee members after a proposal defense are usually conducted behind closed doors, meaning that students receive only a verdict. Without witnessing the process, students are unaware of how the committee arrived at its decision.

Doctoral students erroneously perceive that a dissertation committee is comprised of united individuals—that the committee follows formalized procedures to create a fair process of judging a student's progress with a dissertation; when conflicts arise, committee members discuss the issue calmly, arrive at consensus, and walk away satisfied with the outcome. This perception of unanimity among committee members causes trouble during subsequent stages of a dissertation. It is no secret that politics are common among academicians in the ivory tower, and any conflicts, even those that involve doctoral students, can evolve into grudges and anger that follow a student through the dissertation. Assuming that a committee always operates unanimously, justly, and with a student's best interests in mind skews perceptions of the reality of dissertations. Kaylee found out long after her proposal defense that a part of her proposal was a topic of contention among committee members.

My dissertation proposal was approved shortly after its defense, and all of my committee members congratulated me and wished me luck with the completion of the dissertation. However, when it came time to collect and analyze the data, my chair mentioned to me that I should expect some opposition from committee members regarding the methods I was using. I was shocked to hear this since I passed the proposal defense without any comments or concerns from committee members. I asked my chair for some advice, and he revealed that there was a big argument among committee members during my proposal defense concerning whether the methods I chose were adequate to answer my research questions. I just assumed that the committee members all agreed that all parts of my proposal were sound, or that at least the decision to allow me to proceed with the dissertation was arrived at by amicable consensus.

Luke's success with the proposal defense was a close one:

My committee was comprised of my chair and 4 committee members. After my proposal defense, I learned that the reason for the odd number (i.e., 5 members) was so that votes could not end in a tie. I had no idea that committee members voted on important decisions, such as allowing a student to proceed with a dissertation after the proposal defense and whether to sign the dissertation after the *viva voce*. I always assumed that the chair and committee members arrived at decisions through consensus. At one point, my chair revealed to me that the vote at my proposal defense was three to two in favor of passing. I then realized why I met some resistance while subsequently talking to committee members about my dissertation. I ended up having to juggle a few components in my dissertation, and adding a few new ones, to make all committee members happy.

Dissertation committees operate differently across universities, departments, and even chairs, and there is no way of knowing what goes on behind closed doors during deliberations. Assuming that committee members are like-minded or operate under strict rules of conduct creates the perception in students that unanimity or consensus is the norm when committees make important decisions. Being allowed to proceed with the dissertation after the proposal defense is no guarantee that parts of the proposal will not be questioned later. It is possible that some committee members were not on board with the proposal, or were not in favor of approving it. Expect opposition during every phase of the dissertation, and be prepared to be flexible to accommodate committee members even after a phase of the dissertation has passed.

49
Why Did I Do This?

A good first impression goes a long way, and this advice applies to writing as much as it does to face-to-face meetings. All authors struggle to find the right way to begin a manuscript because connecting with the reader from the beginning sets the stage for how the reader will respond to the remainder of the text. Consequently, the introduction to a dissertation sets the stage for the remainder of the study. It is the only chance a student has to make a good first impression for the dissertation, so a little extra care in the beginning goes a long way.

The introduction to a dissertation is where promises are made and the importance of the dissertation is conveyed to the reader. Saying that the dissertation does one thing and then doing another confuses the reader and might convey a message of deception. Excepting the methods chapter of a dissertation, the introductory chapter is usually the worst written for two reasons. First, students are usually overwhelmed by the dissertation when beginning to write it, and since the introductory chapter is usually written first, some of that anxiety and bewilderment is transferred to the writing of the introduction. Second, even the most well-planned dissertation proposals contain holes because no one can predict how the dissertation will unfold, and even well-laid research plans fall apart during execution. Add to that the fact that the dissertation is being conducted by an inexperienced researcher, and it is clear why the introductory chapter is written so poorly. Essential to writing a good introductory chapter is reporting what the dissertation does, not what you wish it would do. As usual, candidness should guide the writing of the introduction. Elijah made some promises in his introductory chapter that his dissertation couldn't keep:

Writing the introductory chapter was required as part of my dissertation proposal. In it, I discussed that I would develop a model that explains people's behaviors when facing varying degrees of stress. I went into great detail about why developing the model was important to the literature. When I talked to my chair about the model, she pointed out that I was not developing a new model, but instead taking an existing one and adding just a few variables to it. She explained that I was exaggerating what I would be doing during the dissertation, and that some readers, including my committee members, might take exception to not delivering what I said I was doing. I changed the chapter to focus on the importance of the outcomes of the dissertations, and I was more candid with the model I was using.

Owen did not have a clear idea of what his dissertation was contributing before he began writing:

I naturally started writing my dissertation with the introductory chapter, both as logical practice and a requirement of my chair. Unfortunately, I was unaccustomed to scholarly writing at the time, and I was still fuzzy on a few details of my dissertation. To meet the deadline set by my chair, I was more interested in a completed introduction than a good one. Therefore, the chapter made some ambitious claims, including that the dissertation would have a huge influence on my field once we knew the answers to my research questions. I crossed the line from optimism to outright bragging, and it took the advice from more than one committee member to ground me on what my dissertation was really contributing to the literature. Even after the other chapters of my dissertation were complete, I had to revisit the introductory chapter to ensure that I did what I promised.

The introductory chapter to a dissertation is usually the first chapter that a student writes. Without a clear picture of the dissertation, especially regarding what it will look like when it is complete, students often begin promising things that the dissertation cannot deliver. The solution is to take a step back from the dissertation and view it as a whole, rather than an amalgam of individual parts. Vital to the practice is remaining neutral—never over- or under-promising to impress the reader using hyperbole or humbleness. Let the reader decide whether you accomplished the dissertation's goals.

50
Jumping the Gap

The phrase *fill a gap in the literature* is familiar to most doctoral students, and it sometimes haunts them throughout all phases of the dissertation. The problem with the phrase is that it has become mantra, not only pertaining to dissertations, but research that appears anywhere, especially in scholarly journals. Unfortunately, the phrase has lost some of its meaning over the years to a point at which it is a synecdoche, or a small part of something that represents the whole. In this case, the whole is not just the gap itself, but also the importance of the gap and the consequences to the literature or field were it not filled.

I guarantee that no researcher has ever conducted a study to test what happens when cannon balls of increasing size are dropped onto apple pies. I suppose such a study could measure the splatter of apple bits to show a correlation between cannon ball mass and splatter distance. In that sense, there is a gap in the literature. Admittedly, I cannot imagine what literature, but it is a gap nonetheless since it has never been done. This silly example demonstrates that the "it's never been done before" argument is insufficient to fill a gap in the literature. Using that argument, many doctoral students have tried to argue that a gap they discovered in the literature is worthy of study. However, the argument ignores the other parts of filling a gap in the literature—that the literature needs the gap to be filled, and that failing to fill the gap will have negative consequences (i.e., contribute to the literature). Nathan learned that filling a gap in the literature means more than the phrase implies:

> I generally knew what topic I wanted to pursue in my dissertation, but I struggled (like most doctoral students I suppose) revealing the importance of pursuing that topic. I drew heavily from a paper written by a prominent researcher in my field, and I used her model to study a sample

to which the model had never been applied. I thought that that was sufficient to argue the importance of conducting my dissertation. My chair disagreed, and he instructed me to consider what effect my dissertation would have on the literature, if any. Slowly I realized that the dissertation's impact on the literature was a part of filling the gap; I needed to not only fill a gap, but ensure that doing so mattered so that it "contributed materially" to the literature, and did not simply "serve my purpose of being a dissertation topic for me," as my chair put it.

Julian also had trouble interpreting what filling a gap in the literature means:

> There are two competing theories in my field that dominate the literature. In fact, nearly no paper published in the field fails to mention one or the other, or both, when testing relationships between or among variables. My thought was to fill a glaring gap in the literature by testing which theory predicted a shared outcome better, and in doing so put to rest which theory is superior. However, my chair pointed out that even if I did so, the result would apply only to the population I intended to sample for the study; it would not put anything to rest since other results from other populations might yield other conclusions. I learned the hard way that filling a gap means more than studying something in a way that it had never been studied before.

Finding a topic for a dissertation is not an easy thing to do, and discovering a gap in the literature to fill often requires several iterations with the literature of a field. Essential to finding a gap to fill requires understanding that studying something that no one has ever studied before, or in a way that no one has ever studied it, is insufficient. Filling a gap must also contribute to a field by solving a problem and demonstrating the consequences of not filling the gap. In that way, the dissertation fulfills its goal of contributing to a field, not simply adding more evidence to something that the literature has already exposed.

51
Deus ex Machina

Phrases such as *filling a gap in the literature* and *contributing to the conversation in a field* commonly associate with dissertations, and they haunt students who are unsure of how to do it. Doctoral students without a firm grasp of what it means to contribute to a field stumble when discussing the importance of their dissertations, leading them to resort to their own interpretations of what a dissertation is supposed to contribute. Such students default to creating the importance of their studies rather than demonstrating it, using several fallacious devices in a desperate attempt to make a dissertation sound contributory.

The introductory chapter of a dissertation discusses the importance of the study, but students must demonstrate that importance, not create it. Demonstrating the importance of a study means using the literature, and some logic that connects it, to show that the literature is lacking an important contribution, or gap, that the dissertation will make or fill. This sounds clear enough, and most students can easily cite this as the purpose of the introductory chapter. However, scholarly writing is different from other types, especially the enormous amount of popular press and advertising that dominates our lives. Those types of writing are trying to convince us of something, often by exaggerating the benefits and downplaying the disadvantages of an action such as buying a certain car or subscribing to cable service. It is therefore unsurprising that students have trouble operating under the candidness criterion of scholarly writing, which requires writing in dissertations and other scholarly works to be both hyperbole-free and neutral. Exaggerating claims in a dissertation can take many forms, and unless a student is aware of them, he/she is more likely to violate the candidness criterion. Matthew ran into this problem while writing his introductory chapter:

I did not fully understand what was meant by "the literature" when I started my dissertation. I knew that I had to use articles and the findings in them to create a study that contributed to the literature, but I did not realize that I needed to consider all of the literature. I admit that I stopped once I found what I was looking for, and I ended up citing obscure and selected literature to show the contribution my dissertation was making. My chair told me that I had missed quite a bit of important literature, most of which already disproved my hypotheses or answered my research questions. I had to both rewrite the introductory chapter and find a new contribution to make because I had not yet found a gap in the literature to fill.

Connor's problem stemmed from the way he identified a topic:

I thought that I had found a gap in the literature to fill with my dissertation, but I soon learned that the gap was too small. Having struggled with finding a gap, I was excited when I thought I found one, and I was going to make it work somehow because I was not confident about my ability to find another or better one. I used harsh and self-serving language when discussing other authors' publications to show that the gap was both real and important to fill. For example, I discussed that one author had been negligent when constructing a model because he had not included a variable that was important to my study. My chair and committee members rejected the chapter because they said I had manufactured a gap in the literature, not found one.

Finding a gap in the literature is like fitting pieces of a puzzle together, not manufacturing those pieces or manipulating them to fit in a way that benefits you. Think of it as using the studies in the literature, but do not critique them self-servingly. Remember that the studies you cite are already a part of the literature, and they have already contributed to the conversation in your field; your dissertation has not. Improving on past research is one thing, berating past research is something else. When you have truly found a dissertation-worthy gap, you will know it because you should be able to demonstrate the importance of filling it, without needing to ignore literature that contradicts your theories, hypotheses, or propositions.

52
Super Abstract

Parallels between a dissertation and journal article are difficult to draw because the former performs multiple roles and the latter only one—contributing to the literature. They both contain some form of introduction, literature review, methods, results, and discussion sections (or chapters), and they are both written scholarly. However, the length of the dissertation masks further similarities because, for example, the introduction to a dissertation is usually longer than a journal article's literature review. Pressure to fill that space causes doctoral students to guess at what the introduction should contain, which is especially difficult to ascertain since the introduction is usually the first chapter the student writes.

Under pressure to fill the space allotted to the introductory chapter, students shift the introduction from exposing the purpose and importance of the study to summarizing the entire dissertation. They treat the introduction as an extended abstract, and discuss the study's methods, results, and even implications. This is common in textbooks because most of them use the introductory chapter to provide an overview of the textbook's topic, but dissertations do not use the introduction for this purpose. Introductions across major works (e.g., dissertations, textbooks, legal contracts, editorials, etc.) do not contain the same type of information. Since doctoral students are unfamiliar with writing dissertations, they sometimes look to other works to discover what the dissertation's introduction should contain. However, the focus of a dissertation's introduction should be only the purpose and importance of the study, though some universities, departments, and chairs might require additional information, such as formal declarations of special vocabulary used in the dissertation, research questions, and discussions of the dissertation's development. Aruanna treated the introduction to her dissertation as a summary of the entire study:

I boiled my dissertation down to a few sentences that captured the reason I was conducting the study and the importance of doing so. When it came time to write the introductory chapter, I found myself with about a page of text, which included those few sentences. I knew that the chapter needed to be longer, so I began adding any content I could think of, including how I intended to develop the model for the study, what methodology I was going to use, and the results I expected. I still didn't feel that the introduction was long enough so I started discussing the limitations of the study and future research directions. My chair told me that I needed to include only what was contained in those original few sentences, but that I needed to demonstrate how I arrived at what the dissertation was exposing.

Addison's introductory chapter took another form:

I was told that a dissertation's introduction should grab the reader's attention and make him/her want to read more. I misunderstood how to do that, and I instead wrote an introduction that read like an adventure story. My chair said that my introduction sounded like a teaser for a movie; I provided enough to whet the reader's appetite, but not enough to spoil the story. He also told me that the introduction sounded like the reader was about to embark on a journey by reading my dissertation, and that I included far too many details about the study itself, which belonged in other chapters. I referred to a few recent dissertations to get an idea of what a dissertation's introduction should contain, and I was able to rewrite the chapter to fit that expectation.

The length of a dissertation's introduction can throw students off when it comes to what content it should contain, and what it should not. A dissertation already has its own abstract, which includes parts of all chapters of the dissertation. The introductory chapter demonstrates that you are clear regarding the reason you are conducting the study (i.e., the purpose of the study). It commonly includes a discussion of a gap in the literature that the dissertation is filling, and it must show that the gap needs to be filled, not simply that you are filling it. Be especially careful not to use the introductory chapter to state what you are doing in the remainder of the dissertation because that too is only a summary, which is the job of the abstract.

53
According to My Mother

As a dissertation coach, I found that doctoral students do not receive sufficient training on how to search for, interpret, and use articles found in scholarly journals. Most doctoral students know abstractly what the phrase *the literature* means, but do not understand it from a practical viewpoint, which is required to discuss literature correctly in a dissertation. The knowledge that comprises a field is reduced to the synecdoche *literature*, which obscures the larger meaning of the word. A field's literature is certainly more than just words on paper or a computer screen; it represents the process of conducting, reviewing, and publishing research that justifies a study's inclusion in a field's store of knowledge.

Peer review demarks a field's knowledge from other literature that authors produce. For that reason, peer-reviewed journal articles are the primary sources of citations for nearly all scholarly works, including dissertations. This is not to say that other forms of literature, such as books authored by prominent scholars, cannot be cited in scholarly works. However, absent peer review, such sources carry much less weight. Prominent authors commonly compile their findings from their journal articles into books to provide a convenient treatise on a topic, which makes it easier for learners since they can consult a single tome, rather than hunt for articles that span multiple journals. Doctoral students get into trouble when they begin citing findings, facts, statistics, and even opinions found in unscholarly publications, especially those in popular presses such as magazines, newspapers, and websites. There is a pecking order when it comes to the sources that should be cited in scholarly works, and at the top of that order is articles found in peer-reviewed journals. Hannah didn't consider where the information she used in her dissertation came from:

My empirical dissertation dealt with an emerging topic, and so there was little literature on which to draw to justify why I was conducting the study, and to develop hypotheses that could be backed up with solid findings from scholarly sources. My literature review was riddled with newspaper, magazine, and website articles, which was unacceptable to my chair. I realized too late that my topic was perhaps too new to tackle with a dissertation, and I struggled tremendously to find scholarly sources to replace the ones I had used. My advice to doctoral students is to consider whether there exists a strong enough body of literature from which to draw to write your dissertation. If not, don't turn to non-scholarly sources to fill in the gaps.

Wyatt's misperception led to unexpected consequences regarding citing scholarly works:

I guess I must have been thinking old school when I began my dissertation because I perceived that books were more important than journal articles when it came to citing sources. I thought that journal articles were more like research notes that researchers published to move research in their fields forward one step at a time, but that books represented major steps forward, given their length and the time and effort it takes to produce one. Most of the citations in the literature review chapter in my dissertation were books, and when my chair evaluated the chapter, he gave it low marks, saying that I had used the wrong sources for my arguments and propositions. I had to change my thinking when it came to citing scholarly sources in my dissertation, and I had a lot of work ahead of me that kept me busy for several months.

Getting a grasp of what the phrase *the literature* means is required to cite the right scholarly works in a dissertation. Regardless of what you think of periodicals versus books and other sources, journal articles represent the bulk of and most important publications in a field. Before you cite a source in your dissertation, ask yourself whether it represents a major contribution to the field. The most important criterion is whether the work was peer reviewed. No matter how prominent the author, he/she did not need permission from some league of scholars in his/her field to publish a book, write a magazine article, or post an article online. The peer review process functions as a gatekeeper that ensures that only sound findings become part of a field's literature.

54
Let the Reader Sort It Out

The literature review chapter of a dissertation is usually the lengthiest. Its purpose is to demonstrate that what the researcher is doing is supported by the current state of knowledge in a field (i.e., the literature). The primary difficulty that doctoral students have with producing the chapter derives from misperceptions of a literature review's purpose. Some students assume that they know what the chapter should do, how it should be presented, and how it contributes to the dissertation as a whole, and others just start writing and assume that it will make sense once it is completed.

Suppose that you were reading a website article that reviewed a movie you were thinking of seeing. However, instead of critiquing the movie, it gave you a synopsis—an overview of the movie's plot. The problem lies in interpretation of the word *review*, which can mean both *critique* and *view again*. A dissertation's literature review is a critique of the literature, the part of the dissertation that justifies the study's purpose. It is not what I call a *literature pile*, or a place in which an author demonstrates his/her ability to find and cite literature related to a topic. Doctoral students commonly use a literature review to simply report findings from the literature, which admittedly is part of a good literature review. However, they fail to organize the information into coherent arguments that support hypotheses or propositions, and instead pile literature citations into the chapter. The result is a mess that leaves the reader to discern why and how cited literature relates to the study, often creating non-sequitur or underdeveloped arguments. Dylan created a literature pile with his dissertation's literature review:

> By the time I had finished writing the literature review chapter of my dissertation, I had 300 in-text citations and 170 entries in the references section. It took a long time and much work to complete, which led me to believe that I had done of good job of writing the chapter. To my surprise,

my chair and one of my committee members were dissatisfied with the chapter because it did not present arguments that supported my hypotheses and the model constructed from them. I had simply cited findings from the literature, without constructing them into arguments. One of my committee members described the literature review as "shallow," and my chair said that it "looked like a random list of results from other studies." I had to reorganize the entire chapter, remove many of the citations, and construct arguments that supported my hypotheses. I had to enlist help from a writing specialist to get the job done, and it cost a moderate amount to do that.

Elizabeth's literature review took another form:

Deciding which citations to use in my literature review took longer than it did to write the literature review chapter. I was overwhelmed by the amount of research on my topic because the topic was so well-documented in the literature. I tried to include a little of everything, but ended up creating a disjointed picture of the current state of the literature. The biggest mistake I made was failing to develop my hypotheses from the literature. After all of the text I had written that comprised the literature review, I simply wrote something like: "Given the above literature review, the following hypotheses were formulated." I did not develop the hypotheses, I simply listed them at the end of the chapter. I did not know before I began writing the chapter that the literature review was supposed to develop the hypotheses, not simply synthesize the literature.

The phrase *literature review* can be misleading, especially when doctoral students misinterpret what the word *review* means in the phrase. Unfortunately, this is one time when looking to past dissertations does not help because the students who wrote those dissertations might also have misinterpreted what a literature review is, or might have needed to fix their own literature reviews, leaving remnants of the misinterpretation behind. Look to literature reviews that appear in the top journals in your field to see how a literature review should be written. Don't read them for content, but instead for how the literature review is structured.

55
More is Better

A dissertation's length overwhelms most doctoral students, and added to that is the pressure of knowing that the dissertation is being written for a real audience, rather than something shared only between student and professor. It is human nature to impress others, and nowhere is that nature more evident than when a person is being judged. These elements create doctoral students who struggle to produce a lengthy work while trying to convince a chair that the work is worthy of conferment of the title *doctor*. In that state of mind, it is easy to lose track of the big picture.

A dissertation's literature review is a critique of the literature, not a place to simply summarize, synthesize, or report on the literature's past and current states. Most dissertations contain many citations, but the number of citations used in a dissertation's literature review should grow organically, not adhere to some objective ratio (e.g., x number of citations per page) or be used to impress a chair or committee. A doctoral student should use the number of citations that is needed to expose the topic and that represents candidness during exposition of that topic. Doctoral students too often add as many citations as possible, usually for two reasons. The first is to impress the reader (initially the chair and committee members, and later other readers) with the amount of research that went into the dissertation's topic, and second is to mitigate the possibility that literature that should have been included wasn't, applying an *everything but the kitchen sink* approach. Mackenzie fell into the trap of including too many citations in her dissertation's literature review:

> I didn't plan the literature review for my dissertation well enough, and I ended up just stringing together paragraphs that included as many citations as I could fit. Some of my parenthetical citations had 10 or 15 citations in them, which made some of them span more than one line on the

page. I also split many sentences up using citations, resulting in citations making up 60% to 70% of the entire sentence. I thought I was just being thorough, but when I look back at it now, I know that I was just trying to impress my committee. I was in a different place mentally while I was writing the literature review, and it made me blind to what I was doing. I recommend that all doctoral students avoid trying to impress their committees with too many citations because it does not accomplish what a literature review is supposed to do.

Peyton's problem manifested differently:

Before I began work on the final version of my dissertation's literature review, my chair made me write a sample of about 5 pages, what would eventually become the introduction to the chapter. Wanting to get off on the right foot, I included just about every paper from the literature that even vaguely related to my topic. My chair explained to me that there is a difference between being thorough and being pedantic when it comes to choosing which papers to include in a literature review. She explained that I had misinterpreted the scientific method; I should be thorough in my review of the literature, but selective in what I include in it. Once I was on track, writing the remainder of the literature was still difficult, but I was clearer on what the literature review was about. I am glad that my chair made me write that sample before I wrote the entire chapter.

Although you must convince your chair and committee that you have earned the right to carry the title *doctor*, that does not mean that the way to do it is to try to impress them during every step of the dissertation. The literature review is not only the longest, but is also one of the first chapters of a dissertation that a doctoral student writes. Pressure to impress usually manifests in the form of over-citing the literature until the text becomes unreadable. The best way to impress your chair and committee is to demonstrate that you know what you are doing, and no amount of overdoing anything ever makes up for lack of expertise.

56
He Said, She Said

The intertextual nature of conducting and writing up research means that direct and indirect quoting of extant literature is inevitable. The problem doctoral students have with quoting is discerning when to use another author's exact words and when to paraphrase. Many of the most common writing standards that cover scholarly writing offer only vague help with this matter, leaving doctoral students to decide on their own how much of one or the other to use. The result is commonly a dissertation that is pedantic and fatiguing to read because the author used too much direct quoting by default.

Direct quotes use another author's exact words to express an idea in a current work and give credit to the source of the idea, and are usually offset with quotation marks or block text. Most standards also require more than just a citation, so a page number or some other indicator of the location of the quote is required. The problem discussed here is not proper formatting of the two types of quotations, but the choice between them. When exact words are necessary, when there is only one way that an idea can be expressed, or when the quoted author's words were so succinct that the current author does not want to lose the strength of a sentiment to paraphrasing, direct quoting is appropriate. However, some students use direct quoting for the wrong reasons, and in doing so create unattractive or unreadable prose, and signal their nascence with scholarly writing. Others are afraid to paraphrase the ideas of others, and avoid it by using direct quotes. Whatever the reason, the result is an unimpressed chair and committee, and inevitable rewriting. Eli used direct quoting too much in his dissertation, and paid the price in lengthy rewrites:

My dissertation contained an average number of citations for a study in the social sciences, but I made some bad choices when it came to choosing between direct and indirect quotations. I was so afraid of plagiarism, that I figured I would mitigate the possibility by using direct quotes nearly exclusively throughout my dissertation. My chair said that it was unacceptable to do so for two reasons. First, I was avoiding learning how to choose between direct and indirect quotations, a required skill when it comes to scholarly writing. Second, the dissertation was difficult to read with all of the interruptions from quoted text and the addition of page numbers in parentheses. She made me go back and rewrite the dissertation, this time choosing properly between the two types of quotations. That process cost me a few months' time during my program.

Levi used too many direct quotations for another reason:

My chair emphasized expressing the importance of my study, but I admit that I did not know how to do that at the time. I took what I later learned was an authoritarian approach by allowing the words of other authors to express the importance of my dissertation. I thought that the real words from more prominent researchers than me would show the importance of my dissertation better than my own words could do, even were I to paraphrase the ideas of those other researchers. My dissertation looked like a jumble of quotation marks and block quotations, and I had to rewrite it to adhere to the standards that my chair required. Anyone writing a dissertation or thesis should learn when to use direct quotes and when to paraphrase before beginning to write to avoid the problems I experienced during my dissertation.

Doctoral students commonly worry about whether they are producing a scholarly work, but often do something unscholarly in an attempt to be scholarly. Choosing between direct and indirect quotations is a skill that is necessary to master scholarly writing. The best way to learn how to choose between the two is to start by consulting the standard being used (e.g., APA, CMS, MLA, etc.) to learn the rules associated with using quotations. Then look to the top journals in the field to learn how the best authors use quotations, both direct and indirect, to expose a topic. This two-step approach will make the choice between the two types of quotations second nature during writing.

57
Center Stage

A preoccupation with impressing others, especially while being judged, creates affected performers who exaggerate to draw attention to themselves and their accomplishments. This is especially true when people lack efficacy with their performance, and is amplified when rules are discursive, complicated, or unknown. This context describes dissertations well. The default behavior for doctoral students is to emphasize the good in their dissertations and downplay (or misdirect from) the bad, rather than struggle to provide balanced perspectives across all aspects of the dissertation. Nowhere is this more evident than in a literature review.

Discovering a gap in the literature for a dissertation is difficult enough, but then doctoral students must expose the topic scholarly by discussing the gap logically, demonstrating that they have mastered the topic and how filling the gap contributes to the current state of the literature. Not knowing how to do that, some doctoral students use alternate means, often unconsciously, to expose a topic, essentially making up for lack of one skill by using an abundance of another. Suppose that to complete your doctoral program, you needed to run a mile in fewer than 5 minutes. Try as you might, you cannot get under 7 minutes. You might conclude that you can compensate for not being able to run a mile in under 5 minutes by running additional miles to make up for the deficiency. Unfortunately, dissertations—and all aspects of research—do not work that way. In any literature review, mastery of the field and topic must be demonstrated, and cannot be compensated for by doing more of something else. Doing so only prolongs a doctoral program and gives the student a false impression that progress is being made. Grace encountered this problem while writing her literature review:

I proceeded with my literature review unsure of whether I was doing it correctly. I was on such a roll that I didn't stop to check whether I was doing the right thing. Writing argumentatively was never one of my strong points, so I blindly just kept writing, without considering what I was doing. At the conclusion of writing the literature review for my dissertation, I had a wonderful synopsis of the current state of the literature, without having discussed how my topic related to it. My chair was naturally disappointed with the chapter, and I had to stop writing to learn what I had done wrong so I could rewrite the chapter correctly. I don't know why I just kept going. I guess I thought that a sheer amount of writing would somehow make up for not knowing what I was doing, and I am surprised that I allowed that to happen.

Elena unknowingly made up for lack of one skill with another:

My writing skills were more than adequate before I began my doctoral program, but I was unaccustomed to searching for scholarly literature, so my searches returned few results. I thought that meant that the literature was not discussing my topic much, so I endeavored to make the most of what I had. I weaved a tapestry of arguments from just a few threads, and I was proud that I had done so much with so little. When my chair evaluated what I had written, she showed me just how much of the literature I had missed, even some we had discussed prior to my beginning writing. I had to redo all of my searches and ultimately rewrite the entire chapter. I should not have relied so heavily on my writing ability to write the chapter; I erroneously let my creative writing ability dictate what my literature review contained.

Research requires disparate skills, and excelling at each increases the chances that research will fulfill its goals, including completing a doctoral program. Before beginning a literature review, ensure that you understand the skills required to do it correctly. If you find yourself using one ability to compensate for another, step back and ask yourself whether you are doing the right thing, or whether you are simply avoiding the development of the skill you lack. One research skill cannot make up for lack of another, so be honest with yourself and develop the skills you need before you continue.

58
Propaganda

Our lives are bombarded with messages from organizations and people who want our attention, money, support, etc. to further their own goals. What some people call marketing, others call propaganda, but however we classify this inescapable information flow, it is common in our society to never get all the information from those who want something from us. They tell us what they want us to know, and if it matches what we want to hear, we are more likely swayed by the message. Research operates on a different level, guided by candidness during all stages of research.

Researchers must discuss extant theories, methods, and findings that disagree with current arguments, and this candidness is what ensures that research is conducted without personal beliefs or agendas obstructing objectivity. Peer review is one way to ensure candidness and consequently objectivity, and the chair and committee of a dissertation perform this role when evaluating a doctoral student's research. Every researcher has experienced the disappointment associated with developing a theory and then later finding research in the literature that contradicts the theory, forcing the researcher to not only mention that research in the study to uphold candidness, but also rework the theory in light of the evidence found. Some researchers have been caught being uncandid with their exposition of a topic, and that usually means an unpublished manuscript or unfinished (or reworked) dissertation. At some time during their careers, all researchers—including doctoral students—have opportunities to be uncandid to avoid wasting time or money spent developing a theory, and the pressure to do so can be immense, especially when a tenure or graduation decision is on the line. This is when the integrity of the researcher is tested, and the researcher must weigh the consequences should he/she decide to proceed uncandidly. Christian had such an opportunity to be uncandid:

> While writing the literature review to my dissertation, I discovered that research from a related field had reported results that were contrary to what my hypotheses suggested. The research did not show up during my initial literature searches because I did not include the databases that contained them, and I was not expected to have. I faced a dilemma because I feared that I would not only have to discuss the contradictory findings in my own study, but then find some way to justify carrying on with it. I also feared that everything would have to be scrapped and a new topic, or at least approach, pursued instead. I thought about it for a while, and decided to discuss the issue with my chair. Long story short, I did have to change some aspects of my dissertation, but the dissertation only became stronger as a result.

Victoria was uncandid while writing her literature review, and it cost her considerable time to correct:

> While writing the literature review for my dissertation, I knew that I needed to provide a case for the topic I was studying, and for the hypotheses I was proposing. However, I had not searched the literature thoroughly because I later found research that contradicted my arguments, and some research had already covered the topic, albeit using very different approaches. I stuck to citing research that bolstered my topic, approach, and hypotheses, unaware that I needed to consider all of the literature, not just that which fulfilled my needs. My chair looked at what I was doing and told me that I needed to both rewrite the chapter and find a related topic that extant literature did not contradict. The process took me a few months to complete, so I wish I had known about my mistake before I got so far into the writing of the chapter.

Pressure to behave unscrupulously can be overwhelming when a great deal is at stake, and for researchers, that can mean being uncandid to protect time and money spent conducting research. The best way to avoid having to face that decision is to know ahead of time what is expected of you. When it comes to literature reviews, that means being thorough in your searches for literature on your topic and developing a topic from your search results, not deciding on a topic and then finding literature that corroborates it.

59
But Is It Feasible?

Books typically proceed structurally from chapter to chapter, and topic to topic. It is therefore understandable why inexperienced writers begin writing an introductory chapter and assume that since the remaining chapters appear later in the book, subsequent content can be considered once previous chapters are written. However, experienced writers know that chapters in a book are not mutually exclusive; all chapters must cooperate to tell the same story. Consequently, an author must know what a book will look like when it is completed, and that means knowing what each chapter will contain and how it contributes to the story.

A literature review is a critique that sets up a study, especially regarding propositions and hypotheses that will be tested in subsequent chapters. One issue that many doctoral students overlook is the feasibility of conducting a study they promise to conduct in a literature review. Sometimes hypotheses are untestable, propositions undiscussable, and topics too far outside the mainstream of research to provide sufficient evidence to support the purpose or importance of a study. This is especially true during quantitative studies when doctoral students do not consider what needs to appear in the methods chapter to make what's discussed in the literature review possible. Just like a screenwriter or novelist who considers the direction of a story arc (i.e., the trajectory of a story from introduction to conclusion), doctoral students must consider the entire study, even while writing early chapters. A novelist does not begin a novel without knowing where the story is headed, and a researcher similarly does not begin a study without knowing whether it is feasible. Feasibility means knowing what methods are required to carry out a study developed in the literature review. Andrew did not consider the feasibility factor during his dissertation:

I wrote my dissertation chapter by chapter, as my chair required, but I did not make sure that what I said I was going to do in the literature review was possible when it came to execution of the study. I developed 18 hypotheses in my literature review, and other than knowing that I would use structural equation modeling to test the model implied by those hypotheses, I left the methods chapter for later. When it came time to write the methods chapter, I discovered that with 18 hypotheses, 28 relationships among them, and 87 indicators estimating the constructs, the model was under-identified, which means I ran out of degrees of freedom to test the model. I had to rethink the entire model, and in the end, my chair and I agreed that I should combine some hypotheses into more general ones to make testing the model possible. Doing that took considerable time.

Camilla also forgot to assess the feasibility of what she was testing:

I conducted a mixed-methods (both qualitative and quantitative) study for my dissertation that used interviews to discover emergent themes among groups of people who had experienced great losses in their lives, and then used a survey to assess the results that follow such losses. In my literature review, I discussed the 4 groups at length, so they were integral to the purpose of the study. However, when I began planning the methods chapter of my dissertation, I realized that to achieve an adequate degree of statistical power during analysis of the quantitative portion of the study, I needed at least 200 participants—50 per group—but that meant I needed to conduct interviews with those same people, and 200 interviews would be too cumbersome since each would last about three hours. I had to redesign the study to accommodate the needs of the quantitative and qualitative portions of the dissertation.

Books, journal articles, dissertations, screenplays—all text really—proceed linearly for the reader, but not for the author. Writers must consider the big picture and details simultaneously. This means knowing what will come next, and whether what is being written now coincides with what is expected to be written later. When it comes to dissertations, nowhere is this more important than in the connection between the literature review and methods. That connection represents the feasibility of a study. Doctoral students commonly promise things in the literature review that the methods can't accomplish.

60
Filling Unlimited Space

The adage *a job expands to fill the time available to do it* applies in so many ways to dissertations that it is difficult to identify where they overlap. People engaged in long-term projects evolve as projects progress; they get better at what they are doing, and they learn along the way until they no longer resemble the people who started the project. Doctoral students are constantly learning during a dissertation, and they emerge as far better researchers than when they started. That sounds like a positive transition, but there is a hidden paradox—one that is infinitely iterative.

If you are like most doctoral students, the beginning of your program was a time of uncertainty, and there were times when you thought about quitting the program and moving on to other opportunities. Flash forward to today. You are at the dissertation stage, but you can probably think of ways that you would approach earlier stages of your program differently if you could do it all over again. You are wiser now, and less prone to making and repeating past mistakes. However, you can't repeat what you have already done because the program does not allow it. The structure initiated for you was set years ago, before you joined the program, because it serves a purpose and it works well. Conversely, the dissertation is unstructured; it is a time when you will demonstrate your transition to independent researcher, or someone who does not need a structure initiated for him/her. Accompanying such freedom is the possibility that you will not know how to proceed, especially when it comes to knowing when you are done with one task and are ready to move on to another. You must initiate your own structure, and it can be difficult knowing when the structure you initiate is adequate to the tasks ahead. Brayden struggled with initiating a structure for himself:

While writing the literature review to my dissertation, I found myself questioning everything I was doing, which sounds like a good approach, but I didn't know when to stop. By the time I completed the literature review, I was much better at searching for articles, extracting information from them, and using them to develop hypotheses. At one point, I realized that a theory I had previously rejected would have worked better as the foundation for my arguments, but I knew that there was no time to make the change throughout the entire chapter. Instead, I appended it to the discussion, and ended up muddling the arguments I had already made.

The structure Lincoln initiated for himself made it difficult to move on to new tasks:

I was unsure of how to proceed with my dissertation because my chair and committee gave me no help during the first few months I was writing. When it came to the literature review, I struggled no more than most doctoral students do, I suppose, but I found myself daily going back over what I had written the day before and finding ways to improve my arguments, the order of the topics I was discussing, and even the grammar. Half the day was spend rewriting and half spent on new writing. I was proceeding at about half the speed I should have been, and each day I slowed a little bit more since there was now more to rework. I got to a point at which I was at a standstill while I tried to improve the chapter. I realize now that revisiting what I had written would have been better done in chunks, or perhaps the entire chapter at once.

The dissertation that you struggle to produce also produces a better researcher—you. However, that just means you are better able to critique what you just did, and what made you a better researcher, so that iterations of improvement can continue infinitely. Most writers find that they must abandon some writing to move on to other writing, and given the dissertation's length, there is really no other way to proceed with it. Don't get caught up in endless revisions because you are better able to critique your own work. Remember the lessons you learned, and apply them to your next study.

61

Reinventing the Wheel

Creating knowledge does not mean that everything must be produced from scratch. Multiple interpretations of the scientific method agree that current research must build on extant research. Doctoral students often misinterpret having to conduct research that has never been conducted before to mean that everything in a dissertation must be new. However, methods, theories, models, and instruments were developed to allow scrutiny across perspectives and contexts, especially when grounding research in an existing theory or framework. Building on extant knowledge is the cornerstone of research, and chances are at least some research exists on the topic your dissertation is pursuing.

Doctoral students are commonly overwhelmed by the volume of literature that has been published in their fields, and so it is common for them to miss important contributions that relate directly to their own research. Competency with searching for literature combats this, but most graduate programs do not include formal education on conducting such extensive searches, so students must either learn along the way or suffice with the skills they already possess. Inexperienced researchers are also much more likely to satisfice when selecting research to cite or build on. These components combine detrimentally, leading many doctoral students to reinvent the wheel in their dissertations. Although it is true that pure replication of research is not dissertation-worthy, rarely is more than one component in a dissertation new (e.g., theory, method, model, hypotheses, instrument, etc.). The intertextual nature of research means that some research is recycled. A similar problem arises when students are unaware of theories, methods, models, etc. that exist in the literature but that are difficult to find because of a lack of search skills. That's when doctoral students start reinventing and wasting precious time. Natalie experienced this problem while writing her literature review:

> I wanted to study why students choose to either do or not do their home-work, and what effect that choice has on their scholastic achievement. I spent about 6 months developing a model in my literature review that drew heavily from education, psychology, and several behavioral sciences. Developing the model required me to consider not only which variables to include, but also which relationships to include among them. In the end, I had a custom model that tested exactly what I was studying. When my chair evaluated the model, she mentioned that it looked nearly identical to one that already existed. I went to the literature to examine it, and I was amazed at how similar the two models were. I had essentially recreated an extant model, which I could have just used from the beginning instead of trying to create a new one.

Lillian had a similar experience:

> I constructed a model that was similar to ones that appeared in the literature but that added some variables that had never been tested before, which meant there were no measures available for them. I needed to create new measures to accommodate the model. To define the measures, I discussed indicators that estimated the variables as latent constructs to foreshadow their appearance in the methods chapter. My chair mentioned that such measures were available in a related field. I had essentially not opened the scope of my literature searches wide enough to include related fields. There wasn't much damage to fix in my literature review, but I was thankful that creating new measures didn't have to be part of my dissertation anymore.

The best defense against reinventing the wheel in a dissertation is a combination of literature search skills and knowing how to open the scope of literature during those searches. Doctoral students commonly limit literature searches to searching databases, but enlisting help from researchers is a powerful method of identifying the right literature to use. Taking on too much in a dissertation increases the likelihood that it will never be completed. For example, developing a new instrument to use in a model means that a doctoral student must conduct two studies—validation of the instrument, and using it to test the model. The problem is that both studies must produce positive outcomes to contribute to the literature, making completing the dissertation twice as unlikely.

62
Greener Pastures

Methods give doctoral students more trouble than any other part of a dissertation because most graduate programs do not teach enough about research design, or they teach only the theoretical side of methods, exposing students to little to no practical use. For example, being proficient with calculating statistics does nothing to help a researcher interpret statistical results beyond adequate/inadequate or significant/non-significant labels. The result is doctoral students who make methodological decisions based on projections of being able to conduct a study using the methods they know, rather than on what a study requires.

Since most dissertations are empirical, the majority of doctoral students struggle with choosing between quantitative and qualitative approaches. In most doctoral programs, one or the other dominates, predicated on the approach with which professors are most knowledgeable and proficient. Each side acknowledges the other respectfully, but students are still exposed more prominently to one or the other. Those taught primarily qualitative approaches experience more difficulties because the power of using open approaches (e.g., ethnographies, narratives, phenomenologies, etc.) comes at the price of hidden assumptions, and difficulties associated with reliability and external validity. Quantitative approaches also deal with these issues, but they can be dealt with using clearer demarcations of success (e.g., p-values, confidence intervals, statistical power, etc.). Students commonly choose between quantitative and qualitative approaches using unconfirmed information, stories from other students, and half-truths about an approach. Before you hastily choose one approach over another, ensure that you are not trading in one bad experience for a worse one. Lucy chose an approach for her dissertation for the wrong reason:

I chose a qualitative approach for my dissertation because I was never very good with statistics, and I feared having to put my paltry skills into practice. This was especially true since I knew once I made the decision, there was no turning back. I knew very little about conducting qualitative research, but I did know that I would not have to deal with statistics if I chose a qualitative approach. I realized my mistake when I discovered just how complicated qualitative research is, and how many factors need to be considered to ensure validity and reliability. I thought I could just conduct some interviews with a sample of people and look for themes that emerged from them. I had no idea how complicated it is setting up a qualitative study, and I think I struggled more than I would have had I chosen a quantitative approach.

Joshua had a similar experience in the other direction:

My doctoral program centered on qualitative approaches to research but I had an opportunity to pursue a topic that was well-documented in the literature. The topic was lacking some research that I thought was an obvious and easy gap to fill. Since the topic had reliable measures available, and several competing models had already appeared in the literature, the obvious choice was a quantitative approach. I thought that all I needed to do was put the items on a survey, find a sample to take the survey, and let the statistics program calculate the values to tell me whether my hypotheses were supported. However, my lack of experience with quantitative research began to show when I ignored statistical power, chose the wrong statistical tests given the type of data I intended to collect, and didn't know about the assumptions made about population distributions given the statistical tests I had chosen. I struggled greatly to make up for these oversights, and I realize now that I should have stuck with what I knew and had been taught.

The choice between quantitative and qualitative approaches during a dissertation is a big one, but many students choose based on incomplete or incorrect information. Most students are clearly encamped on one side or the other in terms of training and skill, but hop the fence to seemingly greener pastures to chase a single advantage or avoid a disadvantage on the side on which they already reside. Before making a bad decision, talk to experienced researchers encamped on the other side of that fence and learn the truth about the choice you are thinking of making. Anything else would be reckless.

63
The Chicken or the Egg

Doctoral students who conduct empirical dissertations—quantitative or qualitative—must deal with the issue of defining a population and drawing a sample from it. This topic usually comes up only in statistics classes, and is usually glanced over because most formal education in statistics teaches the theory behind statistics and emphasizes calculations, not practical applications. The result is students who do not appreciate the importance of identifying a population to study, or of drawing a sample from it correctly. When it comes to dissertations, treating populations and samples lightly can be problematic.

Doctoral students (and even some experienced researchers) often conduct research backwards, at least regarding some aspects of a dissertation. For example, they identify a sample from which they will collect data, and only then define the population to which that sample belongs. In essence, they do not draw a sample from a population, but define a population using characteristics from the sample from which they intend to collect data. Since populations and samples do not appear prominently in most graduate education, it is no wonder that students define populations and samples obligatorily in their dissertations, rather than as an exercise of sound research. Defining a population lets readers know to whom or what a study and its results pertain. It identifies the context of the study, and allows the reader to determine whether a sample supposedly drawn from a population is representative, and whether conclusions drawn from a sample apply to the population. More than just a task to check off on a list of a dissertation's requirements, defining a population is an integral part of empirical research and should not be taken lightly. Mateo ran into this problem during his dissertation:

I conducted a qualitative study for my dissertation, and as a teacher at a local college, I conducted interviews with students at the college because they were easy for me to access. The sample consisted of 20 undergraduate students at community college X located in city Y in state Z. Since I already knew the sample of students I would be using in the study, I simply defined the population for the study as undergraduate students at community college X in city Y in state Z. I figured that this way there was no way that I could be accused of not drawing a representative sample from a population. My chair disagreed, explaining to me that the population I was really examining was much larger, including future students to whom my results would apply. I read up on the subject, and defined the population more generally to include a wider group of people.

Audrey had a similar problem with defining a population:

During my quantitative dissertation, I sampled a group of managers who had recently been promoted to middle management. I knew exactly which subjects would participate in my study because I had secured them long before I collected data from them. I therefore defined my population as all managers. However, my committee was dissatisfied with this definition for several reasons. The most important was that not all managers make it to middle management, and some were already beyond that level and unlikely to return. The second reason was because promotional decisions are made differently across countries, cultures, and even companies. There were some other reasons, but my committee ultimately made me go back and define a population that my study was observing so that I could better frame the results and who they affected.

The adage *what gets measured gets attention* operates in reverse when it comes to populations and samples in dissertations—*what gets attention gets measured*. Doctoral programs that do not stress the importance of populations and samples in research produce students, and eventually researchers, who take them lightly and discuss them only obligatorily. Just because you identify a group of subjects to participate in a study doesn't mean that it is appropriate to use characteristics of that sample to define a population, even if it guarantees representativeness. Read carefully about the purpose of defining a population in research, and the importance of drawing a sample from one correctly. Treating this topic lightly is the same as conducting questionable research.

64
Eggs in a Basket

Methods sections are difficult to write because few doctoral students receive sufficient practical exposure to methods to allow them to design their own studies. However, universities are not always at fault here because methodology is one of the most expansive and complicated subjects when it comes to conducting research. Consequently, students are often left to do what they think is right, and engage in trial-and-error with a dissertation committee until they get it right, or right as far as the committee is concerned. This is especially common when it comes to finding a sample to participate in a study.

Finding a sample of people to participate in a study can be difficult, and sometimes even after a sample is located and secured, it is taken away because, for example, it would be too disruptive in the eyes of those who granted access to the sample (e.g., managers, leaders, teachers, etc.). Sometimes students depend so heavily on a sample that its removal means restructuring, rewriting, or reconceptualizing a dissertation, or at least parts of it. Some samples are so vital to a study that their inaccessibility means that the study is dead, a very frightening event for a doctoral student. This is why it is prudent to avoid relying too heavily on a sample for the success of a dissertation. Although accessing unique or hard-to-access participants might allow a dissertation to contribute immensely to a field, there is always the danger that the sample might become inaccessible due to timing, withdrawal from the study, closing of a company, new managers, unsecured permissions, etc. Doctoral students should mitigate this possibility by identifying more than one sample that can be used in a dissertation. Makayla ran into trouble with the sample she wanted to use in her dissertation:

As an education major, I planned to survey high school students who attended a local school to assess how their perceptions influenced the types of classes they chose, and my dissertation discussed at length the importance of collecting data from these subjects. For some reason, it never occurred to me that I would not be able to survey this sample. I am a former high school teacher, and I thought that my contacts would make accessing the sample easy. I learned later that to include minors in a research study, I needed permission from the district, the superintendent, the principal, the school's counsellor, the teachers, and the students themselves. The red tape became too thick to cut, and I ended up having to rewrite my methods section and rethink some of the variables in my model to use another group of subjects.

Miguel had a similar problem with accessing a sample:

My dissertation examined managers in organizations, so I received permission from the president of a company to collect data, and we even set a date and time so that I could administer the surveys. On the day of collection, I arrived at the company on time and ready to go. To my surprise, the company was in the midst of a crisis, so this was not a good time to collect data, and no one even knew I was coming. I guess the president of the company figured that I would show up and he would casually get some people to participate. I learned that even when things appear to be set in stone, some people take the task much more casually than you, and there is always the possibility of unforeseen events, like a crisis, that can halt data collection. I had to find a new sample to use in my dissertation.

Doctoral students are too busy to plan for every contingency. However, some contingencies take priority over others, and access to a sample is at or near the top of the list. Even when participants are secured, they can be taken away in the blink of an eye, or perhaps the quickness of an e-mail. Relying on a unique or hard-to-access sample is too dangerous during a dissertation, but even when multiple samples would suffice, don't be surprised if a sample disappears and you must spend weeks or months finding another. Have a plan that includes using an alternate sample if your first falls through.

65
More Eggs in a Basket

Research is expensive in time, money, and opportunity costs. It is difficult for doctoral students to appreciate the cost of research because a university provides nearly all of the resources researchers need to conduct studies at the institution. Your university is footing quite a bill so you can conduct your dissertation. Consider the cost of computers, printers, paper, photocopiers, library services, office space, heating, cooling, maintenance, janitorial services, and too many more to list here. Some statistical software packages alone cost thousands of dollars per user. It is easy for doctoral students to take these resources for granted, and therefore rely too heavily on them.

One of the problems with dissertations is that they are all unique. They might share some similarities, such as methods, models, and theories, but since each contributes uniquely to a field, each is a unique work that can be conducted by only a single person. Consequently, dissertations rely on a unique set of elements to make them possible, even if some of those elements are shared across dissertations. When taking stock of what elements comprise your dissertation, consider the sources of the resources that are needed for you to complete your study. If you find that your dissertation requires, for example, a special piece of equipment, uncommon and expensive software, or a department on campus to run your analyses, you better make sure that those things will be available throughout your entire dissertation, remembering that dissertations always take longer than you think they will. If you are doubtful that the things you will need to complete your dissertation will be available during its duration, find other sources, or plan on using substitutes. Claire had this exact problem during her dissertation:

Everyone in my department used a certain statistical software package to conduct their studies, so I naturally used it to analyze my dissertation's data. I was using the software for months, but one day I couldn't log in to the website that allowed me access to it. It turns out that the university signed a new license with the software company, and students were no longer covered by it unless they paid a hefty licensing fee, and I didn't have that kind of money. Since my data were all in the software's proprietary format, I needed access to that software. One of my committee members allowed me to come to her home office to complete my analyses. I am not sure if that was legal, but since neither the university nor the software company warned us about the change, we figured it was warranted.

Josiah experienced a problem with the hardware he needed to complete his dissertation:

My field of study uses an outdated machine to tabulate results from data. The university owned such a tabulator, and I used it to analyze the data I collected during my dissertation. The tabulator is not accessible to researchers, but is operated by a division of the IS department on campus. When it came time to analyze my data, the IS department was undergoing restructuring, and the university was asked to bear with it as it worked out its kinks. Some services were unavailable at this time, and of course tabulation was one of the services that was backed up. Since I was a student, my analyses fell further and further down the list as professors' needs were prioritized ahead of mine. I had to wait nearly 6 weeks for my results, and I had to graduate a semester later consequently.

When it comes to relying on equipment, software, and other resources out of your control during your dissertation, contingency is the name of the game. Keep a list of the things you need to complete your dissertation, and let your chair see that list. It might go a long way in securing those resources because professors at a university are far closer to being at the center of information than students are when it comes to expiring licenses, expected delays, and other issues that derail research. Explore substitutes and alternative sources of resources, and be prepared by, for example, keeping data in universal file formats and knowing who has external access to the resources you need.

66
Power Play

Statistics are complicated, and so it is common for their purpose and application to be misunderstood, especially among doctoral students who have hundreds of other things to worry about during a dissertation. Unfortunately for the student, chairs, committees, and eventually readers are unconcerned with a student's ability to track all of the important parts of completing a dissertation. What matters is whether the product of a dissertation, including its purpose, methods, and findings, contributes to the literature, and to what degree. Inexperience with research often causes doctoral students to misperceive the importance of some aspects of statistics, only to realize their importance after it is too late.

One aspect of inferential statistics that commonly gets pushed to the back burner is statistical power, or the probability that a test of statistical significance will reject a false null hypothesis. Statistical power has risen in recent decades as a necessary component of what gets reported in research, and its relationship with sample and effect sizes means that researchers cannot consider statistical power only after data are collected and analyzed; it is not an issue of checking whether a degree of statistical power was achieved after analysis, but is something that must be considered before data are collected so that researchers understand how the size of a sample will interact with an expected effect size to produce the probabilities of Type I and Type II errors. Gone are the days of thinking of a large sample as a nicety, but then settling for a small sample due to logistics or cost. Considering statistical power is a prescriptive measure that contributes greatly to the soundness of findings derived from statistical inferences, though some researchers still treat it as an afterthought, if at all. Savannah's experience with statistical power is common among doctoral students:

My dissertation called for me to calculate 22 linear regressions to test my hypotheses. My knowledge was lacking when it came to calculating statistics, so I simply turned to the chapter in my old undergraduate statistics textbook that showed how to calculate linear regressions and followed along until I understood what I was doing. I then used my statistics program to calculate the statistics I needed to report in my dissertation. I guess I didn't read far enough because I was unaware that statistical power was a major issue when it came to calculating certain statistics. I found this out too late, and since the statistical power that my tests had were inadequate, I had to increase my sample size by collecting and analyzing more data. That mistake set me back about two months.

Colton misunderstood what statistical power was used for:

My dissertation had 8 hypotheses that were assessed using regression, so I collected the data and began my analyses, unaware that anything was wrong. I knew about statistical power and what it measured, but I did not know that it was something that needed to be considered before data were collected and analyzed. I conducted a post-hoc power test to assess the level of power of my statistical tests, but it was much lower than conventional cut-offs allowed. I thought that statistical power was just something that was calculated after the F and p-values. In other words, I thought it was another statistic like a standard deviation or measure of skewness that described data and just needed to be reported, not something that affected the ability to detect statistical significance and find support for hypotheses. My chair made me redesign some parts of my study to make up for it.

It is natural that inexperienced researchers are going to make mistakes, but many such mistakes do not necessarily derive from ignorance on a topic; some mistakes derive from a misperception of the level of importance of something. Many doctoral students think that statistical power is an aspect of statistics that is reported obligatorily for the sake of completeness, not an aspect that affects how much data are collected or needed to make sound inferential conclusions. Unlike some other parts of a dissertation, data collection and analysis cannot proceed in a trial-and-error fashion because recollecting data or collecting more data might be impossible, forcing the student to redesign or abandon work that has already been completed.

67
Finders and Keepers

Once a doctoral student knows how to find literature on a topic, what remains is constructing that literature into a coherent study. That description betrays the complexity of a dissertation, but it does capture the spirit of the task. All researchers know that they must cite the sources of original ideas, even if the ideas are not expressed verbatim, to avoid plagiarism and give credit where it is due. However, some original ideas and works cannot be used freely, even if cited properly. This especially includes proprietary material that is not covered by the doctrine of fair use.

Just because something is freely available or easily attainable (e.g., in a library, on a website, published in a journal, etc.) does not mean that people have the right to use it any way they want. For example, a movie producer cannot use a copyrighted song in a movie without permission, which usually involves a royalty payment. Simply citing the source of a work does not grant immunity to copyright infringement. This is easy to forget when citing is so common in research. Some researchers perceive that since they are working for the good of humankind—creating knowledge and disseminating it freely—that they are granted special privileges, both legally and informally, to use whatever they want in any way they want as long as they cite the source. Many researchers have gotten themselves into trouble, and jeopardized their careers and standing in scientific communities, by being careless about how they used someone else's intellectual property. No amount of nascence with research frees a student from liability arising from such infringement, so knowing what is and is not allowed is imperative before beginning to write original works that cite other people's material. Max experienced a copyright infringement issue during his dissertation:

I proposed a model in my dissertation that included constructs that I intended to measure using validated instruments. I was having trouble obtaining the items for one instrument until one of my professors gave me a copy of it from a study he conducted recently. I was glad to have it, and I used the items from the instrument to estimate several constructs. After I defended my dissertation, the manuscript itself had to pass the university's scrutiny, which included checking whether there were any copyright infringements in the dissertation. The university asked me to provide proof that I had paid to use the instrument, and it was then that I learned that use of the instrument required payment. I was lucky in that all I had to do was purchase the instrument to avoid copyright infringement, but it wasn't cheap. I didn't realize that some instruments require payment for use.

Gabriella's experience with using copyrighted materials was more serious:

My dissertation extended an extant model, and so I had to include a history of the model's development to explain my additions to it. Understanding the model requires the reader to view a few figures, so instead of creating my own, or recreating those that already appeared in other studies, I scanned three figures from a paper and included them as figures in my dissertation. I clearly indicated the source of each figure, including the authors' names, the journal, and the volume, issue, and page numbers. I found out later that I needed to obtain permission from the publisher of those figures to reprint them, and I needed to include those permissions in an appendix. I scrambled for a few weeks trying to get the permissions. In the end I did, but if I hadn't, it would have placed me in a bad position with my committee.

The free exchange of information that characterizes a university lulls some researchers into thinking that they have free use of anything as long as they cite the source. However, some proprietary materials require payment or expressed permission to use them, even if they are not being used directly for commercial gain. All researchers should be aware of the laws that govern fair use of copyrighted materials. Many university's offer formal education on the topic. However, remember that even if you were not formally taught about copyright laws, you must still follow them. Ignorance of the law excuses no one.

68

Permission or Forgiveness

A dissertation's proposal can be looked at as a contract; the student promises to conduct the dissertation as the proposal specifies, and the committee approves the proposal, which is the same as saying that the proposal lays out a dissertation-worthy study that if followed, qualifies the student for graduation. The proposal is at least a guide that describes what the student will do and what the committee will accept as a requirement for graduation. However, doctoral students assume that since the committee accepted the dissertation's plan, the dissertation will then not only proceed as planned, but will produce good results. This is not always the case.

Members of a dissertation committee know that research never unfolds as expected, and a dissertation's scope and length only make unexpected or unwanted results more probable. However, it is up to the student to discuss with the chair and committee the contingencies that will protect the student and the dissertation from failure. The adage that *it is better to ask for forgiveness than permission* does not apply to dissertations because deviating from the research plan requires approval from the chair and committee, and such permission usually requires formalities that take the student back to pre-proposal-approval status, which is synonymous with moving backward. Discussing contingencies with the chair and committee is not only wise, it is necessary, but doctoral students too often perceive that sticking with the research plan is sufficient to guarantee success. Like you, your chair and committee have no idea how your dissertation will turn out, so they cannot guarantee that you will succeed. A few uncomfortable conversations before the dissertation proceeds can save a dissertation. Nolan did not discuss contingencies with his chair, and his dissertation suffered as a result:

My dissertation tested only 4 hypotheses, and I say *only* 4 because there were only 5 possible outcomes for my dissertation—all 4 hypotheses were supported (100%), 3 were supported (75%), 2 supported (50%), 1 (25%), or none (0%)—but I did not think of it that way before I began analyzing my data. When I did, I found that only 2 of 4 of my hypotheses were supported, or 50%, and I was concerned that I might not be contributing to the literature enough with just those two hypotheses supported. Since the hypotheses were related, my chair and committee ruled that 50% was insufficient, and that I would have to alter my dissertation and collect new data to continue. I realize now that I should have discussed this issue with my chair before I began collecting data. Perhaps I could have changed the dissertation to include a larger set of possible outcomes to avoid only two scenarios (i.e., 75% and 100%) that would have sufficed as a contribution.

Kylie had a problem with her statistical choice:

My dissertation proposed a model, and I used structural equation modeling to test it. The model was quite large, and when I ran the model in the statistics program, it failed to converge; the model was too big. I knew that this was a possibility all along, but I never mentioned it because I did not want to signal any doubt to my chair or committee regarding my confidence in the study. I figured that if the model could not be run, I would switch to multiple regression and everything would be fine. However, my chair and committee would not allow it, and I ended up having to restructure the model into two smaller ones. I should have discussed the issue with my committee before I committed to the model and using structural equation modeling.

Doctoral students naturally experience apprehension with looking foolish in front of their chairs and committees, but be careful not to allow trepidation to get in the way of obtaining useable results from your dissertation. Contingency is always part of good planning, especially when good results are so vital to success. Your chair might reject planning for contingencies, but better to find out early than regret it later. If possible, discuss your contingencies with a committee member who is open to such speculation, and then use his/her reaction to plan similar conversations with your chair and the remainder of your committee.

69
It Just Has to Work

Over-planning a dissertation is wise since so many things can, and do, go wrong; perseverance is the best predictor of success with a dissertation. However, not everything can be planned, and sometimes returning to the drawing board is the only option. Most doctoral students find that parts of a dissertation must be reworked or abandoned before completion. When planning cannot overcome barriers to success, mitigation of bad outcomes is required, but doctoral students too often assume that outcomes will be positive if no mistakes are made. However, with dissertations—as with all aspects of life—it is possible to make no mistakes and still fail.

No plan is perfect, and dissertation proposals fall into this category. Even the most well-planned dissertations fall apart, and some must be abandoned for reasons that could have been avoided. Some parts of a dissertation can be planned, such as a theory that grounds the research, instruments used to estimate constructs, and statistics calculated to assess hypotheses. Other aspects of a dissertation cannot be planned, such as the suitability of a construct's estimation for use during a statistical test, or the results of statistical tests themselves. The only way to deal with these uncertainties is to mitigate their effects on the dissertation, but most doctoral students do not plan for such contingencies, assuming, for example, that if hypotheses are discussed and grounded properly, they will be supported. Assumptions such as these derail dissertations, and sometimes cost students their chances of graduation. Assessing what can go wrong with a dissertation, and then looking for ways to mitigate the damages, is essential. When you buy car insurance, you pay a premium that gives you the option of obliging the insurance company of buying you out of a bad outcome (e.g., your car is totaled). Buying insurance for a dissertation is more complicated, but it starts by looking for ways to hedge against bad outcomes. Charlie did not consider such contingencies, and it resulted in wasted time and effort:

> One of the variables in my dissertation's model was known to have low reliability (0.75), but it was above the cut-off value (0.7) so I did not worry about it when I collected the data associated with the variable. When I conducted my own analysis on the variable, I got a value below the cut-off (0.58), which was unacceptable in my field. Even eliminating items from the variable did not improve the reliability coefficient, so I had no choice but to find an alternate measure and recollect the data. If I had paid more attention to what coefficients were being obtained in other studies, I would have found another measure, or perhaps not relied so much on the one I used.

Stella experienced a problem with her model:

> The model I tested in my dissertation included a number of independent variables pointing to a single dependent variable. My committee approved the model as part of my research plan, so I thought that all that was left was to collect the data, analyze them, and report and discuss the results. I collected the data, and then I discovered a big surprise as I began to analyze the model. The dependent variable was unusable because the distribution of the data was massively skewed, and it had very low internal consistency. Since all of my hypotheses required that dependent variable, none were testable, and so I could not continue with the dissertation as the plan specified. I had to jump through a lot of hoops to alter the plan, and then I was back to square one with collecting data.

Although dissertation proposals must be thorough, describing in great detail what the researcher intends to do, no plan is foolproof. Before seeking approval for a proposal, doctoral students should perform a what-if analysis, stepping through every aspect of the study before execution to assess what could go wrong and identify remedies. Some remedies are simple, such as switching to an alternate instrument or using a different statistical analysis, but others are more complicated, such as changing assignment criteria for experimental and control groups, or restructuring hypotheses. Overthinking the dissertation is a real possibility here, but underthinking it is far more damaging.

70
It's Got to Be Here Somewhere

Pressure to see a lengthy and costly project through to a successful conclusion causes some people to ignore good practice, consider less-than-optimal alternatives, and even engage in unscrupulous behaviors to avoid big losses. Dissertations fall into this category, and doctoral students are occasionally dismissed from a university due to questionable choices or failure to finish a dissertation in a pre-defined amount of time, often 7 years. Other students are so concerned about failure that they rush to get a dissertation completed, and that usually means making bad decisions regarding research, leading to more serious problems.

Once data are collected, analysis commonly takes only a short time (e.g., days or weeks) to know the results of a study. At that point, a doctoral student knows, for example, which hypotheses were supported, or which themes (if any) emerged from transcripts. Nothing is more disappointing to a doctoral student than when data do not cooperate. Students who obtain close but non-significant results are tempted to consider how to get statistical inferences on the other side of significant. That usually means looking for ways to remove "bad" data from analysis, being liberal with how missing data are dealt with, and getting creative with inferential interpretations, especially justifying higher cut-offs to accommodate data. There might be legitimate reasons to consider such changes, but in most cases, students are not adhering to sound research practices, but are instead torturing data to get them to cooperate. This is especially true when a researcher assumed that results would be positive, and is now looking for a way to make it so. Antonio experienced this pressure when he saw the results of his analyses:

> The most important hypothesis in my dissertation was not supported since I calculated a p-value of 0.052 for it. I couldn't believe how close it

was to being significant, but I needed a value under 0.05. I looked at the raw data and noticed a few outliers, so I eliminated them and recalculated the statistics. The *p*-value was still above the cut-off, so I lowered the threshold for outliers and recalculated, and this time I got a significant value. When I showed the results to my chair, she was initially pleased, but then noticed that the n-size was smaller than expected. She questioned me, and I had to tell her what I did to get the result. She said that what I did was unacceptable, unless of course I had a good reason for doing it. I really didn't, and it was an awkward exchange with her for the remainder of the meeting.

Carson also made some changes to accommodate his data:

I used structural equation modeling to test a model that contained a second-order construct that predicted several first-order constructs. The literature treated 4 latent constructs as indicators of the second-order one in my model, so I naturally followed what the literature did. I obtained poor fit indicators for the model. I didn't know what to do, so I removed the second-order construct and estimated a new one using the raw indicators of the 4 constructs as its indicators. This time I got much better results. However, my committee would not allow it because I could not justify going against the way the constructs were validated in the literature.

Data can be maddening when they return poor results. Rather than step back and see how the problem can be approached differently, or discussing the matter with the chair, doctoral students desperately manipulate data in these cases, sometimes imposing unwarranted restrictions or liberations on analysis parameters to obtain better results. The problem is that the chair or committee members might view this as an attempt to deceive them, and as a departure from sound research practices. Being candid about your results is a priority to avoid bad relationships with a committee. Rather than striking out on your own with data manipulation, consider discussing the matter with an experienced researcher to see if something that lies within the boundary of sound research can fix the problem. At least then you will be armed with an explanation for what you did, rather than look like you tried to manipulate results to suit your needs.

71
Here's What I Just Told You

Some universities provide students with abundant information on how to structure a dissertation, and some provide little to no instruction on the subject. These extremes are common, with few universities situated between. Students whose universities provide a paucity of guidance on what information goes where in a dissertation are left alone to decide on the matter. Looking to past dissertations from the university helps, but the authors of those dissertations were at one time in the same boat as you are now, so they might not have gotten it quite right. The result is a dissertation that lacks continuity, and that often repeats information in odd places.

Most dissertation proposals take the form of the first three chapters of the dissertation—the introduction, literature review, and methods chapters. Dissertations can therefore be broadly broken down into two stages—pre-proposal and post-proposal. The pre-proposal stage is long and difficult because it comprises the bulk of the work that goes into a dissertation. By the time a proposal is defended, it has been months since some of the words in it were written. That makes it easy for doctoral students to misperceive that post-proposal chapters—the results and discussion chapters—represent a new work that is not a continuation of previous chapters. This misperception is exacerbated by the fact that the pre-proposal and post-proposal stages are interrupted by data collection and analysis in empirical dissertations. Consequently, it is common for information in the proposal to be repeated unnecessarily in chapters 4 and 5. It generally takes about an hour to write what takes a minute to read, but this rule of thumb does not apply intuitively to dissertations because some text in them was written months (if not years) earlier, and the desire to reorient the reader with earlier text is strong. Christopher repeated unnecessary information at the beginning of his results chapter:

> My dissertation was empirical, so it included the usual results chapter in which I needed to report the results of my statistical tests and decide whether my hypotheses were supported. However, I was afraid that my committee and other readers would not be able to appreciate the findings unless they were reminded of the significance of them. So, I decided to remind the reader why I conducted the study by restating and discussing in detail all of the major aspects of the dissertation, including the purpose of the study, its justification and link to extant literature, and even the methods. This went on for about 10 pages. My chair told me to remove it because as she put it, "I just read it a little while ago in previous chapters, and my memory is not that bad." We laughed at that one for a while, but I realize now that it makes sense.

Allison repeated unnecessary information in another way:

> My dissertation contained many tables and figures, which my chair and I agreed were necessary to the study's purpose and exposition. Those tables and figures were so integral to interpreting the results of the data analyses that I repeated them so that it would be easier for the reader to interpret the results. Some tables and figures I placed directly into the text, and others I simply referenced again, forcing the reader to flip back many pages to view them. My chair made me remove them because the university's policy did not allow repetition of such elements in a dissertation, and because he said it was a waste of space. My results chapter ended up being much shorter, but it was also easier to read.

Although rarely discussed in the context of dissertations, pacing is a major component in many writing genres, especially fiction. Since so much time passes between some writing sessions during dissertations, students often forget that the length of time it takes to produce text has no bearing on how long it takes to read it. Considering the dissertation from the reader's viewpoint will allow you to more clearly see what needs to be repeated and what would be unnecessary, or even annoying and fatiguing, to the reader. The last thing you want to do is put your chair and committee to sleep while they read your dissertation.

72
Let Me Explain

Writing the results chapter of a dissertation is an exciting time. Assuming that the majority of results from analysis are in a student's favor (e.g., strong themes emerging from transcripts, statistically significant results from quantitative analyses, etc.), it is a time when the light at the end of the dissertation tunnel starts to become visible. While writing the results chapter, some doctoral students are so happy with their results that they enter a state of euphoria, eager to draw attention to and discuss the results. Others are disappointed by their results, and so add information to compensate for them. However, that leads to organizing the dissertation incorrectly, and sometimes leaves little to be discussed later.

The purpose of a dissertation's results chapter is to report results, which means just that—reporting results, not discussing them. This is why the results chapter is the shortest in a dissertation. Results chapters sometimes comprise many pages when dissertations require lengthy or a multitude of tables and figures to report findings, but the text in the chapter is typically shorter than the text in any other. However, a results chapter expands beyond its purpose when eagerness to discuss results causes doctoral students to begin interpreting results in the chapter, rather than simply reporting them. This is a problem because the discussion chapter is where, among other things, discussions and interpretations of findings are presented. This means that interpretations in the results chapter are repeated in the chapter that follows when students let their eagerness get the better of them. Some students also use the results chapter to discuss and interpret, for example, non-significant findings, providing explanations of poor results and even suggestions on how future studies or changes to the design of the current study would yield different results. Liliana used her results chapter to discuss the wrong things:

I was supposed to use the results chapter of my dissertation to report the findings from my statistical analyses. I obtained largely good results, but I guess I wanted to downplay the bad ones and emphasize the good ones, so I included a number of judgements and interpretations of each result I reported. For one non-significant result, I mentioned how interesting it was that the result did not match what I had hypothesized. For another, I expressed surprise, and even offered a brief discussion of the part of the design of the study that might have caused it, as if there was still a chance that the hypothesis was correct even if the result suggested otherwise. I did the same for the positive results, drawing attention to them to emphasize the contribution that my dissertation was making. My chair asked me to remove such language from the chapter, and it was then much starker, but at least the chapter did what it was supposed to do.

Hudson took this practice to extreme:

The results I obtained during my dissertation were disappointing; nearly all of my hypotheses were not supported, and I noticed that the chapter contained long strings of phrases that did not place the dissertation in the best light. I tried to make the chapter more encouraging by pointing out flaws in my hypotheses, and the reasoning behind them. I even went so far as to propose a different conceptualization of my model that might have yielded better results were it testable with the data I had. My committee did not approve of what I had done, but did mention that all of that stuff would make a good discussion in the subsequent chapter.

Dissertations are sometimes guided heavily by university requirements, but beyond such requirements, doctoral students must know what information goes where, and how to avoid unnecessary repetition. Writing the results chapter is an exhilarating experience, but don't let your enthusiasm get the better of you. Be careful not to allow your emotions to take over during writing such that you praise good findings and diminish bad ones to push the dissertation closer to the ideal one you imagined. Findings should be reported in your results chapter without embellishment or alteration, using neutral language to adhere to scholarly standards of exposition. Leave speculation, interpretation, and improvement for the discussion chapter—the dissertation's real discussion of results.

73
Equal Measure

Drawing from experiences with writing in previous courses, doctoral students always ask the inevitable question—how long does my dissertation need to be? They believe that there is a magic number, such as 40,000 words or 150 pages, that dictates when a dissertation is complete. Some students arrive at a target number of words and then divide by the number of chapters in the dissertation to calculate approximately how long each chapter needs to be. Grasping the concept of a dissertation's length is an important step toward finishing one, but some methods are too facile to create practical and accurate perceptions.

Authors of many types of books, such as novels, textbooks, technical manuals, etc., often limit the lengths of chapters that comprise a book to make them generally equal. This is a common practice in the publishing industry that accommodates the experience a reader has with a book. By splitting a book up into equal shares (i.e., chapters), the reader knows approximately how long it will take to read a book, and creates positive perceptions of a book's pace and unfolding of content in it. Unfortunately, some authors force the issue by removing or failing to include important content on a topic, or condensing or expanding text to accommodate a chapter's length artificially, but in doing so create grammatical and structural mismatches between chapters. Dissertation's are different from most types of books in that they serve a special purpose—contributing to the knowledge in a field. Consequently, they do not follow such rules of length, but instead adhere to scholarly standards that revolve around candidness. Bulking a dissertation's chapter to follow a rule regarding length falls outside of the candidness standard. Cooper experienced a problem with the length of his results chapter:

The results chapter of my dissertation was shorter than the previous chapters, even though I included everything in it that was required. It was less than half of the next shortest chapter, and it made the table of contents at the start of the dissertation look lopsided. I didn't want my committee to think that I was being negligent with the chapter so I looked for ways to increase its length. I added some longer descriptions of my constructs instead of using abbreviations, and I began the chapter with a summary of the methods. I realize now that I made a mistake because my committee made me return the chapter to its original length. My external advisor explained to me that the chapters in a dissertation need to do what they are supposed to do, and should never be held to arbitrary principles such as length.

Pablo took his misperception to a higher level:

The model I constructed for my dissertation took a lot of space to develop in the literature review, but testing it was simple. This meant that the results chapter was very brief, barely over 10 pages. I didn't think that the chapter was long enough, so I increased its length in what I now know is a strange and redundant way. I can sum it up with an example sentence from the chapter: "Variable A correlated positively with Variable B, which means that as Variable A increased, Variable B increased, and as Variable A decreased, Variable B decreased." It is so obvious to see now why such a sentence is redundant, but at the time it made sense to me. My chair made me remove similar redundancies, and I am glad to say that they did not make it into the final version of my dissertation.

Doctoral students want to perform their best with each chapter of a dissertation, but some chapters call for one type of exposition and other chapters call for another. Self-imposed (and imagined) standards and misperceptions about the purpose of a chapter cause students to make some strange choices. Worrying about length is common during a dissertation, so getting comfortable with a dissertation's size is a first step to getting the content right. If you find yourself doubting whether you've done enough, discuss the matter with your chair or a committee member. There is a good chance that doing so will subside your concerns and keep (or place) you on the right track.

74
Fatted Calf

Like baking a cake, dissertations require the right ingredients, and in the right proportions, to ensure that the product fulfills its goals, in this case contributing to a field's literature. However, some cakes require a certain ingredient, and others do not. In parallel, some dissertations require the inclusion of some elements, and others do not. Doctoral students stray from the purpose of a dissertation when they start including elements for the sake of including them, especially due to some arbitrary perception. They commonly misperceive that it is better to have something and not need it, than need it and not have it. Conservatism takes over, and they start overcompensating, usually to the detriment of the dissertation's exposition.

Tables and figures are common elements in scholarly manuscripts, dissertations included, which add a layer of understanding for the reader that text alone cannot offer. However, it takes some skill to know when a table or figure is required, when it would be superfluous, and when it would just confuse the reader. The ubiquitousness of tables and figures in research makes some researchers believe that excluding them from a study is unscholarly, and that they must find some way to include at least one of each. This is especially true among doctoral students who are fearful that they are forgetting something in their dissertations, and so they throw some in for good measure. Completeness is a relative term when it comes to dissertations (and really all forms of research), and knowing when a study is complete takes experience, which doctoral students lack. Sometimes being a good researcher means knowing when not to do something, and overcoming the pressure to include unnecessary tables and figures in a manuscript is a good example. Callie struggled with this issue during her dissertation:

I didn't pay too much attention to the need for figures in my dissertation because I seemed to be getting along just fine without them. When I was writing the results chapter, I looked to extant literature in the journals and dissertations authored by past students from my university to get an idea of what I needed to do, and I noticed an undeniable constant; all of them contained figures. I would have felt like my dissertation were too dissimilar from them if I didn't include some, so I looked for ways to force one or two in. The first opportunity I found was a figure that was a pie chart of my sample's gender composition, but it ended up being just a simple dichotomy, with 42% male and 58% female. I included a few more charts that were similar, but my chair said to remove them because they added no more clarity than the text already offered.

Dolores struggled with the tables she added to her dissertation:

The structure of my dissertation was such that I had many research questions to answer, so I naturally thought that the best way to do that was to state a question and then answer it. However, I used the same logic when it came to the tables that supported those answers. I included many tiny tables, most of which consisted of two columns and a single row. My chair advised me to combine the tables into a few larger ones because the university, and the writing standard I was using, requires that a table have at least two columns and two rows. Combining the tables also made it easier to lay out the document since the university imposed several requirements on the placement of tables, such as no table was allowed to appear at the top of a page.

Visuals such as tables and figures organize information for a reader in a way that makes understanding content easier. The adage *a picture is worth a thousand words* applies in research, especially when space is at a premium, such as in a journal. Within reason, dissertations have far fewer restrictions regarding length, and that freedom causes doctoral students to be careless when it comes to what elements to include and exclude in a dissertation. Knowing when something will help a reader and when it is being included arbitrarily is vital, and such discernment is the mark of a researcher.

75
Ho-Hum

A discussion section in scholarly manuscripts is the most misunderstood component during exposition of a study. It is unsurprising that doctoral students struggle to understand the purpose and importance of a study's discussion because even experienced authors treat it lightly and misunderstand it themselves. Some authors espouse a discussion as the most important part of a study, and others include it obligatorily because it is expected and a study is incomplete without one. However, the discussion chapter of a dissertation is an opportunity to demonstrate to a chair and committee that the transition from dependent student to independent researcher has occurred, and therefore should not be taken lightly.

Discussion chapters of a dissertation are often written hastily for two reasons. First, most doctoral students are rushing to complete the dissertation because they are trying to meet a cut-off date for submission. Since the discussion almost always comprises the final chapter of a dissertation, it is written quickly and is not given the attention it deserves. Second, doctoral students are impatient when it comes to finishing a dissertation, wanting so badly for it to be over that they start sacrificing quality for completion. This also means that the discussion does not receive much attention. However, the discussion of any study addresses the big picture, especially regarding what it all means and how findings add to the literature. Most discussions also identify research that logically follows from the present study. Such components of a discussion demonstrate that the student understands how the dissertation fits within current literature, though most treat such sections as obligatory, not as opportunities to demonstrate learning and growth as a researcher. Doctoral students forget that the product of a dissertation is a researcher who is capable of acting independently, not simply a study that contributes to the literature. Adrian misunderstood the importance of a dissertation's discussion chapter:

> I was running out of time to submit my dissertation for final approval, and I still had most of the discussion chapter to write. I worked on it over a weekend, and at its conclusion, I had enough content to qualify as a chapter. However, my chair told me that the chapter was too vague, and it included only generic statements that discussed the importance of the study. I basically said that the findings were important, future research is important, etc. I checked on it and it turns out that I used the word *important* 43 times in the chapter. I had to rewrite the entire discussion, but first I had to learn how to write one, so it was a long few weeks. I also missed the deadline and had to reschedule both my defense and graduation date. I should have given myself more time to complete it, and knew what I was doing before I attempted it.

Reagan's perception of a dissertation's discussion took a different form:

> I was taught early in my education that every good piece of writing includes a good conclusion, so I thought that the final chapter of a dissertation was its conclusion. I used the chapter to summarize the entire dissertation, including restatement of the purpose of the study, research questions, hypotheses, literature review, methods, and findings. Nowhere did I discuss the significance of the findings, and neither did I talk about research that still needed to be conducted. I was dismayed when I found out that the entire chapter needed to be trashed and rewritten, but I realize now that I should have been more careful about my assumptions.

Rushing to get something done that is not fully understood is a dangerous way to proceed with anything. Doing so especially tricks authors into thinking that shortcuts are a good idea (e.g., rush-to-solve bias), and that some of the text that they write is good enough (e.g., self-deception). It is therefore surprising that doctoral students would ever proceed this way, but it is nearly universal because dissertations are always rushed to completion. Before you find yourself in that situation, learn long beforehand what a discussion chapter should contain and how it is exposed in writing. You might not know the content of what you will write about in the chapter, but at least you will know the form it will take.

76
Ad Nauseam

What content is supposed to appear in a discussion section has perplexed researchers since discussions became a requirement when reporting research. Bombarded with bad examples that appear in journal articles and other students' dissertations, doctoral students struggle to construct coherent discussions in their own dissertations, and often misuse the discussion chapter by including just about everything except a discussion. A discussion section or chapter is not simply an obligatory component when reporting research, and it should not be taken lightly, especially by students who are trying to convince a committee that a dissertation is complete.

The chapter titled *discussion* in a dissertation is an abbreviation for *discussion of results*, but most students misinterpret what a discussion is, and they guess at what content the chapter should include. Imagine that a salesperson showed up at your door and tried to sell you a vacuum cleaner 1950s style. The salesperson tells you that the vacuum is the best available, and you are intrigued so you ask for more information on what makes it the best. Instead of providing the information you asked for, the salesperson simply repeats how great the vacuum is. Misunderstanding what a discussion of results is supposed to do, doctoral students similarly repeat information, but do so by altering the language used to repeat it so it sounds different. A *discussion* of results is not a *reporting* of results; that's what the previous chapter was for. Instead, it is a discussion of the larger implications of the results of a study, including what influence the results will have on future research, and to whom the results are pertinent. Sophie misinterpreted what a discussion chapter is supposed to contain:

> I saw the discussion chapter of my dissertation as a wrap-up of the study; it was there so that the dissertation didn't end with the results chapter. I

found myself flipping back to the chapter that was on results to find things to write about. I followed the flow of the results chapter so well that I had made a facsimile of it, just stated in different ways. The chair of my dissertation said that the chapter was unacceptable and that I would have to write it again, this time making sure that the discussion was about the results, not the results themselves. It took me a long while to figure out what to discuss in the chapter, and since I hadn't planned on the chapter taking that long to write, it held up my graduation by about two months.

Alysa also repeated her study's findings in the discussion chapter:

I had a lot of problems delivering a satisfactory discussion chapter to my chair, and I sensed his impatience with how long it was taking. I thought that the best way to write the chapter was to state a finding from the dissertation and discuss it, and then do that for each finding. Eventually I sought help from a writing specialist, and she showed me that once the restated findings were removed from the chapter, I had only told the reader how important the findings were, but I didn't discuss the findings in any way. She literally cut all of the findings that I repeated in the chapter and showed me what remained. As she put it, the writing was shallow, and I needed to include more substance in the discussion.

Reporting the findings of a study and discussing them are two very different things. The discussion section must do the latter while keeping the former to a minimum, though reminding the reader of the finding being discussed is warranted if ambiguity is a possibility, and to give the chapter structure. To get the hang of it, write a few pages and then remove all of the content in those pages that repeats what appears in other chapters of the dissertation. This way you can see the original content of the sample. If what remains is shallow—it says almost nothing of importance—then you are relying too much on repeating what's in previous chapters to fill the discussion chapter. At that point, rethink what you are writing about, and discover what the purpose of the chapter is before continuing and creating more problems.

77
Everyone for Themselves

Pressure to complete a dissertation is strong throughout its entire duration, but one area particularly fraught with pressure is developing arguments that demonstrate the importance of the study. During the proposal stage, doctoral students commonly spend months constructing a study that contributes something to current literature. That pressure subsides after a proposal is defended and the study is underway, only to resurface when it is time to finalize the discussion chapter. Rather than discuss what contribution the study will have on the literature, the student must discuss what contribution the study makes now that the results are known.

The phrase *contribute to the literature* is familiar to all doctoral students, especially when discussing problem and purpose statements early during a dissertation. The idea is that a student cannot simply conduct a dissertation and then let the readers figure out for themselves what the value of the study is. Students must be clear about what a study accomplishes, and demonstrate that those accomplishments are important to the literature. While writing the discussion chapter of a dissertation, those contributions are no longer theoretical because the results of the study are known, and the student must find a way to demonstrate that the study was not in vain and that it makes a contribution. When trying to do so, doctoral students commonly proceed unscholarly, attempting to market the study to the reader using a hard-sell approach. The result is more than unscholarly exposition; it is a chapter that exaggerates the study's contribution, often at the expense of extant literature. Students forget that they and their studies are not competing with other authors and the literature that those authors create. However, pressured to espouse the importance of their dissertations, doctoral students temporarily turn colleagues into competitors. Jeremiah used a hard-sell approach in his discussion chapter:

After a few failed attempts at the discussion chapter of my dissertation, my chair suggested that I concentrate on the contribution my study was making to the literature. I didn't know how to do that, so I began writing about the superiority of my study in comparison to those already published in the literature. I started by gently discussing that my sample was better than any other used to examine the topic in the literature, and that my design was the best so far because it isolated variables in ways that no other author had done. I kept doing this for every aspect of the study, but I wasn't paying attention to the overall message of the chapter because I was too focused on the details. The effort ended in another failed attempt, and I had to start again when my chair rejected what I had written.

Francisco took the practice to extreme:

My dissertation's results were great; all of my hypotheses were supported and statistical results were strong, which is contrary to what the literature usually reports. I let my results go to my head because I used the discussion chapter to point out deficiencies in extant literature. I went so far as to suggest that the topic of my study be left to those specifically trained to study it, and that studies from those authors be scrutinized more carefully for faulty logic and bad research designs. My chair pointed out that my study drew heavily from much of that extant literature, and that the only thing more suspect than a faulty foundation is anything built on such a faulty foundation. I was humbled by the experience, and immediately started writing a new discussion chapter for my dissertation.

Research is not a competition; it is a contribution. The intertextual nature of research suggests that extant studies represent foundations of current and future research, and that even when past research is found faulty, the literature would not be where it is without such mistakes. When writing the discussion chapter of your dissertation, avoid judgmental words and phrases that either explicitly or implicitly suggest the superiority of your dissertation over extant literature. When comparisons must be made, choose words carefully, and demonstrate that the arguments, design, and results in your dissertation add to extant literature, rather than supersede it.

78

Intralink

The chapters of a dissertation demark its major portions, but they still work in concert to identify, develop, and address a research agenda. The way most students approach a dissertation, especially thinking of chapters as milestones to completion, means that doctoral students commonly treat each chapter as its own project. This is easy to do since it is difficult to keep the purpose of a long-term project in mind when bogged down by details and daily tasks, making it important for students to consider the purpose of a dissertation before writing each chapter.

The discussion chapter of a dissertation brings the entire purpose of the previous chapters—and therefore the entire dissertation—into focus, not by summarizing or recapping, but by discussing the contribution that the study makes to the literature. Prior to the results of a dissertation being known, all contributions that a dissertation makes to the literature can be discussed only theoretically. However, after the results chapter is written, and the results of the dissertation are known, the real contributions of the study can be discussed simply because they are now known. Linking findings to the purpose of the dissertation is vital because doing so demonstrates that the dissertation has fulfilled its intent. Equally important is discussing how the dissertation fell short of contributing to the literature in the way the author thought that it would, before results were known. In combination, the successes and failures of the dissertation to fulfill its purpose reveal its contributions—the real ones. This is an opportunity for a doctoral student to demonstrate that the transition from student to researcher has occurred, and that the dissertation is complete. Asher did not link his dissertation's findings to its purpose:

I erroneously thought that since some of my propositions in my dissertation were not supported that the dissertation had failed to fulfill its purpose. I was concerned that such results would be unacceptable to my chair and committee, and that I might have to collect and analyze new data. I needed a way to show that my dissertation had fulfilled some purpose, even if not the one it set out to fulfill, so I focused on some ad-hoc analyses in the discussion chapter. I did discuss the original propositions and their results, but I quickly followed them with the ad-hoc results to show that even though I didn't find one relationship, at least I found another. I was put at ease when my chair told me that the results I got were acceptable, but that I needed to position them more prominently in the chapter since they were the findings the study set out to obtain.

Eleanor did not link findings with the purpose of her study in a different way:

The results of my dissertation were disappointing, and when it came time to discuss those findings in the discussion chapter, I wanted to demonstrate that a bigger contribution to the literature was being made than the results suggested. So, I developed a new purpose for the study—one that fit better than the one I discussed in the dissertation's introduction. My chair said I couldn't do that because it would be like shooting an arrow into the air and drawing a target where it landed. The dissertation's findings had to be discussed using the purpose I wrote about before I knew the results. I rewrote the chapter, and my committee was pleased with the way I discussed the path from purpose to results.

The desire for good results in a dissertation is strong, especially when students perceive that the difference between good and bad results is tantamount to graduating and not graduating. Some doctoral students divorce the link between the purpose of a dissertation and its results if it draws attention away from the fact that the study did not entirely fulfill its intent. However, no study is perfect, and studies do not always fulfill their purposes as planned. That is not a weakness of the research process, it is its strength. When writing the discussion chapter of your dissertation, create a strong link between the purpose of the study and its results. That is the best contribution that your dissertation can make.

79
Interlink

The term *literature* takes on a life of its own during dissertations because doctoral students not only draw from literature to create a study, they also contribute to it. The literature seems like a looming entity that is difficult to define, grasp, and conceptualize, and as a synecdoche, the word encompasses more than it conveys. Students rarely perceive the seriousness of contributing to literature for two reasons. First, the dissertation is usually the student's first attempt at research that is not for a fake audience, and second, students place the literature on a pedestal as something to admire, not something to critique or change.

When a doctoral student begins a dissertation, the literature takes a new form—that of medium to mold and create new knowledge, much like a sculptor uses clay to mold a new artistic construct. This description might seem out of place when scientific research is the topic, but it demonstrates that the literature is no longer just something from which to learn; it is a collection of knowledge from which new knowledge springs. Most students see the literature as a tool—something to be picked up and used when needed, and then discarded or placed aside when no longer useful. Consequently, it is common for doctoral students to miss the larger picture when it comes to how their dissertations contribute to the literature. They see a dissertation as a lone study to be judged by a committee, and as an indicator that once accepted, signals the completion of the program. The result is both the inability to see how the dissertation contributes to the literature, and difficulty relating extant literature with the dissertation's contribution. This makes writing parts of the discussion chapter more arduous. Austin experienced trouble relating his dissertation's findings to extant literature:

One requirement for my dissertation was that I had to show how my findings contributed to the literature in my field. I didn't know what that meant, but I thought that the best way to do that was to state what findings were in the field already, and then restate my findings so that the reader could compare them. Rather than return to the literature, I used what was in my literature review to reiterate what was there. I then restated my findings from the previous chapter. That's what showing how my findings contributed to the literature meant to me. However, my chair told me that restating any part of the dissertation was not allowed. I had to create original content for the discussion chapter that dug into the larger meaning of what my dissertation contributed. I struggled with it for a long time before I got it right.

Louis also did not understand what it meant to demonstrate a contribution to the literature:

Throughout my dissertation, my chair emphasized knowing what contributing to the literature means. Unfortunately, it lost all meaning for me because he emphasized it during every aspect of the dissertation. When I began writing the discussion chapter, I was concerned when he told me that this was the chapter in which I needed to drive home the contribution my dissertation made. Instead of showing how my findings fit within extant findings, I discussed gaps in the literature generally. I then repeated my findings, without relating them to the gaps I had discussed. My chair told me that I had identified the wrong gaps, but that if I identified the right ones and related my findings to them, I would be on the right track.

Juxtaposing a dissertation's findings and findings from extant literature is not the same as demonstrating the contribution to the literature that a dissertation makes. Neither does simply identifying gaps that are unrelated to the current study's findings. Think of a discussion of a study's contribution to the literature as fitting puzzle pieces together. Two identical pieces can't fit together, but neither can dissimilar pieces whose contours are not complementary. The idea is to identify what gaps in the literature exist, and how the dissertation's findings fill them. However, unlike in other chapters of a dissertation, identification of fit alone is insufficient. What's needed is a discussion that explains the importance of the fit, not only that a fit exists.

80
I'm Sorry

Beyond the gap being filled, a dissertation's methods, data collection techniques, statistics, and many other components affect the contribution made to the literature. This is one reason that all aspects of a dissertation are scrutinized so heavily at the proposal stage, and why students must spend so much time developing the proposal. Dissertations should not evolve; unless a fatal flaw is discovered, they proceed as the proposal lays out. However, lack of flaws when planning a study does not mean that the study will contribute adequately to the literature, and discussing such flaws is required in nearly all fields.

No study is perfect, but many journals and dissertation committees reject manuscripts that do not include a candid discussion of a study's limitations. However, doctoral students commonly misunderstand the purpose of a limitations section, and instead use it as an excuse to design a study that either fits within their current range of knowledge or makes things easier on themselves to avoid complicating a dissertation. Keeping it simple is a good idea when it comes to any study, but making it simple when the literature needs something more complicated does not accord with good research practice. A dissertation—any study really—must address a gap in the literature that needs filling, not one that is convenient for the researcher or whose only purpose is mitigating a bad research outcome. Discussion chapters in dissertations often do not state and discuss limitations; they apologize for ones that were unnecessary. Doing so demonstrates that the study could have been designed better, or could have offered a greater contribution to the literature had other samples, designs, statistical calculations, etc. been used in lieu of the ones chosen. Ezra apologized for an unnecessary method she chose during her dissertation:

When I was designing my dissertation, I assumed that the more complicated it got, the more that things could go wrong. One choice I made based on this assumption was using the same people to collect both independent and dependent variables. I could have collected the two types of data from different sources, but by not doing so, I introduced the possibility of single-source bias. I figured that I could treat that choice as a limitation of the study, and that all I had to do was mention it in the limitations and recommend that future research use multiple sources of data. My committee raised some concerns and made me go back and run some new analyses to test for single-source bias. That set me back about 5 weeks, and I realize now that a little more work during data collection would have saved me precious time at the end of the dissertation.

Chase's committee also had some issues with the limitations of her dissertation:

A limitations section was required in the discussion chapter of my dissertation. My study examined behaviors across perceptions of companies. In the limitations section, I mentioned that I should have considered collecting data at multiple companies to avoid homogeneity of perceptions from a higher-level of analysis (i.e., the company level), which of course couldn't be tested because all participants worked at the same company. One of my committee members mentioned this at a pre-defense meeting, and there was some discussion of whether this limitation was a problem that required more attention. I thought it would be enough to mention the limitations of the study, but I did not think that I would be expected to act on them.

The limitations section of any study is not a place to apologize for limitations, as if being candid about the limitations of a study excuses any degradation of the contribution the study makes to the literature. When planning a dissertation, anticipate explanations or excuses you might have to mention in the limitations section, and assess whether you have good reason to include such limitations in the study. Some doctoral students use the limitations section of their dissertations as a catch-all for all the things they should have done differently. Apologizing to the reader does not make everything alright, and it might prompt a chair or committee member to rethink what you did with your dissertation, and whether it warrants remedial actions or more serious corrections.

81
Opportunity Knocks Loudly

Discussion chapters in dissertations across many fields typically contain similar sections pertaining to a study's findings, including implications to research, implications to stakeholders, limitations of the study, future research directions, etc. Although these sections are separate, they relate a similar story—how the study contributes to the literature. However, just because they are separate does not mean that they do not or cannot serve as inputs to each other. The most prominent opportunity for such a relationship is overlooked by many doctoral students, causing them to struggle unnecessarily with writing the chapter's content.

The future research recommendations section in a dissertation's discussion chapter is a chance to demonstrate that the doctoral student has a grasp of the literature that extends beyond the current study. It shows that the student's understanding of the literature has developed into being able to identify what future research is needed to contribute even more to the field. However, identification of future research must be in relation to the current study. One area overlooked as a potential source for future research recommendations is the limitations section. Limitations are more than just a list of aspects of a study that would have been nice to avoid, and they are more than limitations that are common to all studies. Assuming that they were unavoidable in the dissertation, limitations represent aspects of a study that might have influenced the results, and that might have led the researcher to the wrong conclusions. The best way future research can build on the current study is to find ways to remove the current study's limitations. Researchers who provide ways of overcoming current limitations in future research contribute even more to the discussion. Mia ignored her dissertation's limitations when writing her future research recommendation:

My chair and the university's dissertation guidebook offered few details on what I needed to discuss for future research recommendations in my discussion chapter, save for the requirement that I include such a discussion. Therefore, I didn't know what I was supposed to write about. I used the section to discuss research other than my own dissertation that I thought that the literature needed. I essentially discussed gaps in the literature that had nothing to do with my dissertation, including ones I thought I might fill with my dissertation but later rejected when I was writing the proposal. My chair informed me that I needed to discuss future research that should be conducted given my dissertation and the findings I discovered with it. It all makes sense now, but I wish I knew that before I spent so much time writing about the wrong things.

Annabelle's future research recommendations were diminished by her dissertation's discussion of limitations:

I didn't put much thought into the limitations of my dissertation because I assumed that since it was approved and guided by a committee, comprised of experienced researchers, and agonized over by a worrisome doctoral student that there were no major limitations to discuss. So, the limitations I wrote about in the discussion chapter were generic. For example, I mentioned that the data were gathered from only one institution, and that they were analyzed using a single statistical test. To be honest, I included the section only because I had to. My chair told me that mentioning those limitations were acceptable, but that I needed to consider the limitations specific to my study that might have interfered with its findings. It took me some time to get my chair to accept the future research I recommended, but I got it right in the end.

Doctoral students must identify the limitations of their dissertations, but those limitations should not solely be those common to most studies in the field. Were only common limitations used to recommend future research, all recommendations in the literature would be identical across studies. Just like a dissertation is a unique contribution to the field, its limitations and the future research recommended from them must also be unique to the dissertation. Connecting current limitations with future research recommendations is a powerful tool while writing the discussion chapter, but failure to do one well means that the other also suffers.

82
Don't Blame Me

Worrying about whether their dissertations are contributing to the literature is common across doctoral students studying any field. Contributing to the literature is a central theme in all dissertations regardless of the topic or methods used to expose it. Pressure to demonstrate a contribution is so strong that some doctoral students engage in hedging, exaggeration, and even unscrupulous behaviors to clarify a contribution. It therefore comes as no surprise that students are reluctant to discuss anything that dismantles the contribution they fought so hard to construct, and when forced to do so, commonly find ways to lessen the blow to their contributions.

The limitations section of a dissertation is difficult for doctoral students to write because it seems counterintuitive to mention limitations when the entire manuscript revolves around convincing readers, especially a chair and committee members who are judging the dissertation, of the contribution the dissertation makes. Mentioning limitations appears to be a kind of reverse marketing, like a company recommending that you don't buy its products by showing the disadvantages you would experience if you did. However, discussing limitations accords with the candidness principle of research, wherein researchers are forthcoming about the negative aspects of their studies so that readers, especially other researchers, can create informed judgments of a study's contribution. Researchers under pressure to demonstrate a contribution often lessen the impact of limitations by either describing them euphemistically or leaving the most offensive ones out of the discussion. When forced to discuss limitations, it is common for doctoral students to structure writing to mitigate limitations as negative aspects of the study, especially by mentioning the dissertation's strengths, hiding limitations among positive topics, and blaming the literature for allowing similar limitations. Emilia tried to lessen the impact of her dissertation's limitations:

> I dreaded writing the limitations section because it seemed strange to have to simultaneously show that my study was making a contribution to the literature and that it contained limitations to making that contribution. I prefaced the limitations section with a reminder to the reader of the contribution my dissertation made. Much of what I wrote was a repeat of what I had discussed earlier, even drawing from parts that appeared in the introductory chapter. I even reminded the reader that all studies have limitations, and that judging my dissertation based on its limitations would be unfair since even studies in the best of journals have them. The original draft of the section went on for about a page before I even mentioned the first limitation. My chair made me remove that preface so that only a discussion of the limitations themselves remained.

Xavier's limitations section took a different form:

> I was already concerned that I had not demonstrated well enough in previous chapters the contribution that my dissertation was making, so I was especially concerned about discussing the limitations of my dissertation in the final chapter. Therefore, I refuted each limitation, hoping to lessen the perception that my dissertation even had limitations to discuss. For example, I mentioned that I had ignored a variable in my model that had recently appeared in the literature, but then I countered with the argument that the variable was new and was untested. I countered the limitation that my sample size was small by arguing that I was a doctoral student and didn't have the resources to obtain a larger sample. I countered all of the limitations this way, but my committee made me remove them and leave only the limitations.

If you think that mentioning limitations is counterintuitive to garnering positive perceptions of a study's contribution, you are in good company. Researchers are pressured to diminish negative perceptions of their research, and they use many writing devices to lessen their impact. Journals commonly reject papers until limitations are discussed properly, or at all, and dissertations are often delayed until a student does the same. Discussing limitations is a part of research, and researchers who know that they must discuss a study's limitations are apt to design better studies to avoid awkward discussions in a limitations section.

83
Let's Get This Over With

The defenses associated with a dissertation (i.e., the proposal and dissertation defenses) share some similarities, but it is their differences that get doctoral students into trouble. One misperception that students commonly hold about the proposal defense is that it is a formality—that the defense would not have been scheduled did the chair and committee members perceive that the student were not prepared to defend. Students are often shocked by the experience they have during the proposal defense as a result, and the same is true of the dissertation defense.

It is common for doctoral students to view the dissertation defense as the last hurdle to the completion of the dissertation, and although that is true, the dissertation defense is much more. The proposal defense is about assessing whether a study is viable; it is as much an evaluation of the proposal as it is an assessment of whether the student is capable of carrying the study through to completion. In contrast, the dissertation defense is about assessing the student as a researcher, not one who is about to undertake a dissertation, but one who must be capable of conducting research independently, without the watchful eyes of a chair and committee. Consequently, the dissertation defense is about evaluating a much more serious topic than whether a dissertation was conducted as planned, and a mistake now might lead to conferring a degree on someone who does not deserve it. That alone demonstrates that the dissertation defense is not and cannot be a formality. Many doctoral students do not end up with a signed dissertation after its defense, having to recollect and reevaluate data, add new sections to the dissertation, or rewrite sections that are inadequate. Overpreparing for a dissertation defense is nearly impossible because anything can and does happen. Aarav was surprised by the turn his dissertation defense took:

I was confident going into my dissertation's defense because I believed that I had prepared well and I was ready to answer tough questions about my dissertation and its findings. After I presented the dissertation, the floor was opened to questions from my committee. One member asked me about my readiness to conduct research on my own, and about my plans to conduct research once I graduated and found a position in academia. At first, I took the question lightly, and I provided a general answer about wanting to conduct research. However, the committee members started asking even harder questions on the same topic, and I didn't have any good answers planned. My dissertation was approved, but I was surprised that the defense was not a cut and dried experience.

Kelly also found out that the dissertation defense is not a formality:

I discussed my dissertation with my chair before I defended it, and since she said that it was time to schedule the defense, I assumed that I was ready to complete the dissertation and graduate. However, during the defense, my chair asked me to evaluate my own development as a researcher, and how much I had learned during the dissertation. One committee member asked me whether I felt I had transitioned to a researcher and someone capable of conducting research once I graduated. I felt cornered because I thought that the outcome of the dissertation was set; I would defend and that would be it. I had to schedule another defense that focused on me as a researcher, not so much on the dissertation itself.

Thinking that a dissertation's defense is a formality is common because it seems strange that a defense would be scheduled were a student expected to do poorly. Part of this misperception derives from the hectic time between the end of writing the dissertation and the defense's date. Not having much time to prepare for a defense makes students perceive that it will be easy, as in a formality, since that's what they need. If possible, try to schedule some time before the last chapter is written and the defense is scheduled to take place. Rushing to finish the dissertation and then rushing to prepare for the defense means that many things can go wrong, even if it is just a misperception of the dissertation defense's purpose.

84
Lateral Learning

Preparing for anything in life is always easier when you've experienced whatever it is you are preparing for. This makes preparing for a dissertation defense difficult because it is rare that someone experiences more than one in a lifetime. Talking to former students, reading books (even this one), and getting advice from committee members are wise strategies, but those sources of information are poor substitutes for experiencing a defense yourself. Given the inability to experience a defense before you defend your dissertation means that some things must be left to chance. However, you can mitigate the worst of them by doing one simple thing.

Most universities offer multiple doctoral programs across many fields, and that means that at any given time, there are at least a few dissertation defenses scheduled for the near future. At 4+ years to a doctoral program, several dozen or more dissertation defenses probably took place during your residency at the university. It is surprising then that it never occurs to some students to attend at least one or a few such defenses. It is true that some universities, and the departments within them, hold closed-door defenses, the reasons for which are many. However, most defenses are open-door, or require only the permission of the defending student's chair to attend. Whatever the case, witnessing a defense is the next best thing to experiencing one for yourself. If you do attend a dissertation defense, pay little attention to the topic being discussed and focus on the format. Watch for how often the student is interrupted so a committee member can ask a question, and be mindful of the types of questions being asked. In essence, the topic being discussed is less useful to you than how it is being discussed. Harrison attended another student's defense, and he learned a few things about his own:

I had the opportunity to attend another student's defense. I was busy but made the time to go because I was interested in the topic of the dissertation. The process of the defense was surprising to me. Each committee member was given 10 uninterrupted minutes to ask the student questions, and once the time was up, the next committee member got his/her 10 minutes. This continued until it was the chair's turn, but the chair was not limited to how much time he had to ask questions. I talked to the chair after the defense, and he told me that most defenses on campus operated like this so that each committee member got a chance to voice concerns, and so that no one was able to dominate a student's defense. I asked my chair about it, and she told me that my defense would proceed similarly.

Zane also learned about his own defense by attending another's:

My chair recommended that I attend an upcoming defense of a dissertation so that I would know what mine would be like. I attended the defense and found out that it was like a conference presentation. The student did not initially present anything because the committee was already familiar with the dissertation. Instead, the student was asked questions and then had to answer them by giving a brief presentation on the topic. My chair described it as a conference approach, where the student had to defend the dissertation only by answering questions from the committee members. Anything not asked by the committee was not part of the defense. My chair told me that this approach streamlined the process and ensured that only issues that concerned the committee members were addressed.

Dissertation defenses can take many forms, but the standard presentation style is the most common. However, it is unwise to assume the format that a defense will take, and even if a defense follows the standard format, there might still be some idiosyncrasies specific to a university, department, or chair that would be unwise to discover after your defense has begun. Attending other students' defenses, especially those of the students in your cohort, is the best way to learn about such idiosyncrasies. Don't assume that your chair or committee will inform you of the format your dissertation defense will take. Find out for yourself by attending a few before yours is scheduled.

85
Rote Sufficiency

The anxiety associated with an imminent dissertation defense is a time when doctoral students take stock of their dissertations and ensure that they understand everything about them. They want to appear confident about the dissertation, but at the same time don't want to come across as too confident; it is a time of conflicting emotions and much second-guessing. Doctoral students perceive that the best way to combat these extremes is to know their dissertations even better than the chair and committee members do so that no questions or concerns will go unanswered or unaddressed. However, this focus on the dissertation is what derails students during a defense.

Demonstrating expertise is more than knowing a lot of facets about a topic. It involves understanding the larger picture in which a topic is embedded. Memorization is not a viable means to demonstrate mastery of a topic, and doing so emphasizes that mastery has not been achieved. When it comes to a dissertation, memorizing its contents does not equate with mastery of the topic it discusses; it only means that the student has the ability to memorize something. A dissertation defense is not simply a recounting of a dissertation's topic; it is an opportunity to demonstrate that a student has mastered the topic sufficiently to contribute to its development. Consequently, doctoral students should be prepared to discuss why the dissertation is a contribution to the literature, and why it signifies that the student is ready to function as an independent researcher. Chairs and committee members must be able to gauge this transition, and to do so, they ask tough questions and bring up complicated subjects during a dissertation defense. How well the student answers and addresses them determines success or failure with a defense. Karabou had to answer a tough question at his dissertation defense:

During my dissertation defense, and on behalf of the entire committee, my chair asked me to explain how well my dissertation fit within the current state of the literature. He said that the question was wide open, and that I could answer it any way I felt would do the job. I began answering by discussing the gap in the literature that my dissertation filled, but my committee and chair wanted something else. They wanted to know less about the gap that my dissertation filled and more about how well it filled that gap. My first inclination was to be modest to maintain conservatism about my dissertation's effect on the literature, but my committee encouraged me to speak freely and say what I wanted to say. The conversation got candid quickly, and very uncomfortable. I got through it, but it was a difficult conversation to have during an impromptu discussion.

Zachary also had to answer an uncomfortable question during his defense:

During my dissertation's defense, my committee asked me to pretend that I was back developing the proposal, and to reimagine the study. In other words, what would I do now that I couldn't and didn't think to do back then? It felt like I was being asked to sabotage my own study by identifying how my dissertation was not as good as it could have been. My chair later reminded me that I am a better researcher now than I was when I started the dissertation, and that the question was designed to demonstrate growth as a researcher. I wish I had known the motivation behind the question when I was answering it, but I see now why a committee would be concerned about a student's growth as a researcher, and self-assessment reveals much on that topic.

Having to answer tough questions is common during defenses, but it isn't possible to prepare answers to them because that too is just memorization. A person capable of conducting research independently is someone who has mastered a topic and can discuss it without much preparation. Some questions and conversations during a defense extend beyond the dissertation itself to include the larger picture of the dissertation's place in the literature, and conducting research generally. You can't prepare answers to questions you don't know will be asked, but knowing that they are possible during a defense shows that you must master your topic, not just memorize it.

86
The Best Laid Plans

If doctoral students learn anything from a dissertation, it is that anything can happen, and sometimes it does. Murphy's Law always operates during all dissertations, and any plan can fall apart at a moment's notice, including losing access to a sample of participants, results that don't support hypotheses, and altered requirements at the seeming whim of a chair. By the time students reach a dissertation's defense, you would think that they would be prepared for anything, but a few issues still sneak up and derail a defense, leaving the student vulnerable.

The linear presentation, or lecture, is the most common pedagogical tool, found at all levels of education. Electronic slides, a largely linear presentation format, are so common in institutions of higher learning that it seems strange to attend a lecture or even a dissertation defense and not be subjected to them, and they fit well with linear learning. Most students prepare electronic slide presentations for their dissertation's defense, and it is good practice because going it alone, without an aid to keep a message on track, is dangerous and unnecessary, and creates bad impressions among attendees. However, relying on electronic slides means that doctoral students must ensure that the technology needed to run and display them is in place during the defense. Blaming the university's IT department that the application or hardware needed to use electronic slides is little comfort if a doctoral student must proceed with a defense sans the electronic slide presentation that he/she prepared for the occasion. It also starts the defense off on a bad note, and in extreme cases, compromises the defense. Bella discovered the problem with relying on technology being available where it once was:

> I was relieved when my dissertation's defense was booked in a room in
> which I had been teaching for several semesters. I was familiar with the

room's layout, and I knew what software was available on the computer there. On the day of my defense, I inserted my USB drive into the computer, but noticed that the computer did not recognize the file for my electronic slide presentation. I figured it was a glitch, so I clicked on it anyway and the operating system said that the file was unrecognized. I restarted the computer but got the same effect. I learned later that the university was involved in an upgrade of the software it licensed, and that some computers that couldn't be updated remotely wouldn't have the software available until someone installed it manually. Before I knew it, my chair said that we should reschedule the defense, and people started filing out of the room.

Jordon also had trouble with technology during his dissertation's defense:

My defense was scheduled in a lecture hall across campus in a classroom normally used by other schools on campus. I assumed that the electronic slide software that is available on every computer I have ever used on campus would be available there, but I found that some departments on campus used open-source presentation software, and the one I needed was not on the computer in that classroom. My file wouldn't open with that software, and I had to continue without it because the university does not allow connection of personal laptops to the network. It was awkward continuing without the presentation I had created, and I and my committee had to refer to printouts of the dissertation throughout the defense.

Reliance on technology and Murphy's Law go hand-in-hand. Before showing up for your dissertation's defense, consider everything that could go wrong with the computers, software, and projection hardware available in the location that the defense is scheduled to take place. If possible, do a dry run of your presentation just before the defense so you can test whether everything you need technology-wise is working properly. If you think that something isn't quite right, have a substitute standing by, or request a room that has more reliable technology. Have your electronic slides available to you in multiple media (e.g., USB drive, cloud storage, etc.), and consider bringing hard copies of the presentation, enough for each committee member, in case everything goes wrong and you have to proceed old-school.

87
Rubber Stamp

Experience is a powerful teacher, and as researchers, doctoral students should be familiar with the concept that although past evidence is a good predictor of near-future phenomena, no amount of evidence can guarantee that something will or will not happen. This is especially true when aspects of a dissertation occur multiple times. For good reason, doctoral students are universally apprehensive about a dissertation defense, and it makes them look to the past to ease their minds about an impending unknown. They rely too much on what little evidence from the past they have, and they pay the price after it is too late.

The two defenses associated with dissertations share some similarities; they involve the same people, deal with the same topic, and can result in multiple outcomes. However, the purposes of the two defenses are very different. Proposal defenses tend to be more informal for two reasons. First, proposals are scrutinized heavily during their development, and committee members are consequently more familiar with them when they are defended. Anything can still happen, but it is more difficult to reject what you were a part of. Second, proposals do not represent the final word on whether a student graduates; there is always time later for a committee member to withdraw support of a graduation recommendation. Demeaners during dissertation defenses are more conservative because committee members do not want to make a mistake, and once a recommendation for graduation is given, it can't be withdrawn easily or humanely. Conservatism increases drastically during a dissertation defense. Consequently, a doctoral student's experiences with the two defenses can be very different. Julia experienced this during her two defenses:

> The defense of my proposal was shockingly informal. It was scheduled just a few days in advance, and my committee members took me out to dinner

to celebrate afterward because they told me immediately that the proposal was approved. I was pleased but bewildered at the informality of the whole thing. That is why my dissertation's defense was equally shocking, but in the other direction. That defense was highly formal. It was scheduled far in advance, and during the defense, everyone had serious faces and seemed to concentrate on every word I said and answer I gave. I didn't mind it, but I still cannot believe how different my dissertation's defense was from my proposal's. Even the report that my dissertation had been approved was delivered solemnly. They still took me out to dinner to celebrate, but it took me a few hours to make sense of what had happened.

Tristan also noticed differences between his defenses:

My proposal defense went something like this: I discussed every aspect of the study from beginning to end. I started by informing my committee of the problem statement, the purpose of the study, and the assumptions I was making while conducting the study. I proceeded to discuss the justification for the hypotheses and model I was testing, and then the methods I would use to gather and analyze the data. I concluded with projections of the results I expected, and the implications of those findings to current and future research. I was allowed to proceed methodically, and I preferred it that way because there were no surprises. However, when I defended the dissertation, the committee wanted to focus only on results. I had a whole presentation planned, including a recap of the entire dissertation. I don't know how we did it, but we ended up discussing the results of my study for nearly two hours.

Proposal and dissertation defenses serve different purposes, and by the time a dissertation is defended, committee members are very familiar with it, and require fewer reminders on what the dissertation's focus and purpose are. The final defense represents the last time that committee members can avoid making a mistake by graduating an undeserving student, and consequently, things get more formal and serious during that defense. This is not to say that committee members are commonly whimsical while assessing a proposal, but when a dissertation's completion is far in the future, it is easier to give a student some room to make mistakes and learn from them.

88
Down in Front

During a dissertation, doctoral students must constantly match what they have control over with what they can't control. In fact, the struggle a student goes through in trying to create such matches is what determines success or failure. With some aspects of the dissertation, it seems like the student has a firm grasp on the situation, and at other times it feels like being at the mercy of a raging river while being pulled through the rapids. There are times when making peace with the unknown is the only option, and one of those times is during the dissertation's defense.

Dissertation defenses take many forms, and even those planned to proceed one way have a way of deviating to a degree that they no longer resemble what was planned. It is common for defenses to evolve as the student presents the contents of a dissertation, usually determined by the questions that committee members ask and how well the student answers them. Some aspects of a defense cannot be planned by either student or committee, and students must be engulfed in a defense before they know the format it will take. Sometimes even just the mood of the committee members can change how a defense proceeds. Students' efficacy also plays a role in how a defense unfolds, and there is always the question of who's in charge during the defense, the presenter or committee members? There is one constant across all defenses—anything can happen. One aspect of defenses that students are unprepared for is just how involved they will be during the defense. It is intuitive that since the student is defending the dissertation, he/she is the center of attention, but that is not always the case. Some defenses proceed without much input from the student at all. Abdul was surprised that his dissertation defense seemed to have nothing to do with him:

About 15 minutes into my dissertation defense, a committee member asked me to stop to ask the chair a question. From there, more questions were directed at the chair, and he continued to answer them. The questions, which eventually turned into a conversation among the committee members, went from specific to general, from questions about samples and statistics to the merit of the dissertation. The defense now resembled a post-defense deliberation. I was eventually allowed to continue, but after answering just a few questions, I was asked to leave so that the committee could discuss the dissertation in private. A few hours later, my chair congratulated me on a job well done; my dissertation was signed and complete.

Keira felt like an observer at her own dissertation defense:

My dissertation defense was going as well as to be expected, but it changed instantly when one of my committee members asked a question related to my methods. Another committee member chimed in, and then my chair started in. It became obvious to me that the method I had used in my dissertation was a topic of contention among the committee members. I stood quietly at the front of the room, waiting for a signal that I could continue, but it never came. By now the discussion among the committee members turned into a kind of negotiation, almost as if I had nothing to do with my own dissertation. When the defense ended, I learned that I needed to add some minor statistical calculations to the dissertation at the insistence of one of the committee members. I never understood exactly what happened at the defense, but it seemed to have more to do with my committee members than with me or my dissertation.

The format of a dissertation defense can be planned, but there is no guarantee that it will unfold that way. Remember that a dissertation committee, especially the chair, is very familiar with a student's dissertation, largely because committee members are given time between a dissertation's completion and its defense to read it. This means that they do not need a play-by-play presentation of the dissertation as if they have never seen it before. Dissertation defenses are not formalities; the committee members are there to critique both student and dissertation, and some just want to get to it.

89
Center of the Dissertation

Doctoral students think that they are on their own to complete a difficult task, and that is true to some degree. The focus is on the student, and that makes students think that they stand alone at the center of the dissertation—they are the only ones affected by its success or failure. This perception is flawed, though it is understandable how such perceptions develop during a dissertation. However, misunderstanding who else has a stake in a dissertation leads to conflicts among stakeholders, and that means that dissertations are sometimes held up until all stakeholders are satisfied.

Although they do not produce the dissertation, chairs and committee members are stakeholders by serving those positions. They have responsibilities to the university, and even have emotional attachments to a dissertation. For example, seeing a student through a doctoral program is a source of pride for professors. Doctoral students are not cheap; universities have a lot invested in students during their residencies. Universities are also concerned about the reputation that former doctoral students will develop for themselves and their alma mater, which can reflect on the university both positively and negatively. The point is that there are many people and entities who have a stake in the doctoral student's dissertation, and like the student, each stakeholder is being pulled in different directions based on what's being measured and who's watching. Unfortunately, most of the pressure associated with fulfilling all stakeholders' concerns and requirements falls on the student's shoulders, whether the student is aware of it. That means that some parts of a dissertation and some behaviors by the actors involved seem strange or arbitrary to the student, and some stakeholders' motives reveal themselves only near the end of a doctoral program. Easton learned of a hidden stakeholder while defending his dissertation:

My dissertation defense went about as normal as I guess one could, and I was wrapping up my presentation when my chair asked me a question to which I did not know the answer. She asked how my dissertation would reflect on the university, and whether I thought the university was satisfied with my dissertation. I answered as well as I could, trying not to sound overly confident. I was too curious not to ask, so I questioned my chair after the defense why she had asked me that question. She told me that the dissertation affected not only me and my career, but outcomes for several people, even the university as a whole. She had asked the question to see what my reaction would be, and to remind me that there is more at play than whether I do or do not graduate.

Bailey witnessed an unexpected conversation among committee members during her defense:

During my dissertation's defense, some of my committee members started steering the topic toward whether my dissertation had fulfilled the needs of the university, but not in a way that had to do with meeting requirements, such as length, rigor, quality, etc. It had to do with whether the dissertation was something that the university and committee members would be willing to put their names on. It was as if we—the university, the committee members, and I—were creating something to be marketed. I created the dissertation, and I had the most to gain or lose by either finishing or not finishing the program. I guess everyone, even the university, had something to gain or lose, though I never thought of it that way.

Dissertations are larger than doctoral students perceive, and rarely are they aware of how far they reach and how many people they affect. When nearing the end of a dissertation, individuals and groups seemingly appear out of nowhere to ensure that a dissertation meets standards and is ready to be called complete. It is easy to resent people and entities who seemingly had nothing to do with a dissertation when they suddenly start judging it and testing its suitability to meet disparate standards. However, this is the nature of a university, and its system of checks and balances does more good than harm, even though it might not seem that way when so much is at stake for a student.

90
Apology Denied

The relationship between a dissertation's proposal and the dissertation itself changes over the course of a dissertation. The proposal represents a plan that when carried out, will allow construction of a complete study. In that sense, the difference between the two blurs because one is an input to the other. However, plans change to adjust for unforeseen circumstances, and the importance of following a proposal rigidly is subjugated to contributing to the literature and producing the best study possible. Students often fear having to deviate from a dissertation's proposal, and try to compensate for it during the dissertation's defense.

The dissertation proposal is a kind of contract between student and committee that represents what the student promises to deliver and what the committee agrees to accept as a dissertation. At the beginning of the dissertation process, the proposal is rigid in that deviation usually requires permission from the chair and committee, and perhaps even a formal presentation to justify the changes. Later, especially when students begin collecting data, proposals are sometimes found to be flawed because the student, and even the committee, did not anticipate the logistics of collecting data the way the proposal required, or could not anticipate circumstances that arose after the proposal was approved. During such revelations, the proposal becomes more malleable because there is no reason to proceed with a dissertation that cannot be conducted, or produce a dissertation that contributes little to the literature. However, some students are apprehensive about deviating from the proposal, even when given permission to do so, because they perceive that it represents a failure on their part to design a viable study. This apprehension carries over to the dissertation's defense, where students apologize for deviations unnecessarily. Sora felt that she had to explain the changes to her proposal during her dissertation's defense.

> The research design that appeared in my original proposal called for me to sample a certain group of people randomly such that I had a true experimental design. However, when I began collecting data, it became obvious that I could not assign subjects randomly into the experimental groups. Data collection stopped so that I could discuss it with my committee, and we decided that I would switch to a non-random, quasi-experimental design. I was disappointed because I believed that the switch diminished what my dissertation was contributing. During the dissertation defense, I mentioned the switch many times, and even felt bad that I had not lived up to what I had intended to do. My chair gently told me during the defense that I could let that issue go, and that I should concentrate on what my dissertation did, not what it didn't.

Elliot was disappointed by a deviation between proposal and dissertation:

> My dissertation tested a model that related several independent variables to a single dependent variable. I learned that I would not have access to the information I needed to collect the dependent variable, and the proposal needed to reflect a new focus on a different, though related, variable. I knew that the new variable was not as important as the original, but I had no choice but to proceed with it. Before my defense, I asked my chair whether I should mention the original variable or pick up where the altered proposal started. She said that although she agreed that the original variable would have made a greater contribution to the literature, there was no need to discuss it in that manner. She did recommend that I mention the variable as a possibility for future research.

Proposals appear unchangeable from the moment a committee approves them, and most committees do not allow deviations without formal procedures. However, committees recognize that the unforeseen can halt research, and once that happens, the only two choices are to cancel a study or change it. When proposals change, doctoral students feel required to apologize, and that they let their committees down or that the changes reflect poorly on the student as a researcher. However, research plans are never followed blindly. Committees know that changes are inevitable and that the experience will benefit the student in the long-run.

91
But We Never Discussed That

Dissertation defenses seem so finite; a student either does well and gets a signed dissertation, or doesn't do well and must remediate it. That dichotomy between success and failure means that most doctoral students become conservative when preparing for the defense. The idea is that by doing exactly what is expected of them, they have the best chances of creating a positive outcome. On the surface, that advice is sound, and it works in most situations, even those outside of dissertation defenses. However, the problem is not with the conservatism, but with whether students know what is expected of them.

Anything can happen during a dissertation defense, but most doctoral students assume how the defense will go, sometimes without much thought. Most students assume that the defense will proceed orderly, including a time when the student will talk uninterrupted, and that there will be a period during which committee members will ask questions. In essence, the defense is misperceived as a formality. Doctoral students commonly create electronic slide presentations for the defense, and assume that the presentation will proceed linearly. These assumptions represent what students think is expected of them, but it is easy being conservative about such mundane expectations. The expectations that a student does not anticipate is what derails a dissertation defense, which requires both being able to think on your feet and planning for contingencies. The former can only unfold during the defense, but the latter can be anticipated. Some students prepare a very rigid and pithy presentation, and end up running out of material to present. Others are afraid of talking too much, and wanting to get the defense over with quickly, leave too much on the cutting room floor when preparing their presentations. Parker found that his defense's presentation was lacking in substance:

I spent a lot of time planning how my dissertation defense would go, and I was lucky in that I knew ahead of time that I would be allowed to present my dissertation without interruption from the attendees. When I finished presenting, I realized that I had spent only about 20 minutes talking about my dissertation, and I had run out of slides to present. This surprised my committee since I knew how the defense would go. I spent the remainder of the defense having to discuss new topics off the top of my head. I knew that it was not going well, but I had no choice but to carry on and return to some previous slides to fill the time.

Gianna also experienced a problem with presenting at her defense:

When I was preparing my electronic slides for my defense, I spent days deciding what information to include and what to discard. I must have created about 100 slides, but I narrowed them down to about 30. I over-estimated how long it would take me to present those slides, and so the defense moved forward very quickly. I wish that I had had some of those slides back so that I would have had something to turn to when I ran out of slides to discuss. Learn from my mistake and make sure you have more to discuss than you think you will need, even if it means going into minute details about your dissertation. At least then you will have something to discuss if the defense moves quicker than you thought it would. Never underestimate how much you need to prepare for a dissertation defense.

Unlike other aspects of the dissertation where the adage *more is less* applies, the defense's motto should be *more is more*. Don't plan on discussing every detail of your dissertation, but be prepared to do so if necessary. Always have at least a few extra slides at the end of your electronic slide presentation that you can turn to if you need to discuss more. Also, keep a hard copy list of what slides are where, and number them, so you can flip to them directly, without having to flip through each to get to the ones you need. You can never overprepare the content of a dissertation defense, so give yourself the best chances of success by being prepared to discuss anything that might come up.

92
Stop the Presses

Even after a dissertation defense is complete, and the dissertation itself is signed, there remain a few more hurdles for a doctoral student to traverse. In comparison to the defense, they appear minor, but that doesn't mean that they can't hold up a graduation, and in extreme cases, jeopardize it. One task students forget about is formatting the dissertation to the university's, graduate school's, and thesis office's standards. Before you count on your degree, be sure that you are aware of any standards with which your dissertation must comply before the university will hand over your diploma. There is much at stake even after a dissertation defense, so take such final tasks seriously.

All universities require students to submit final versions of their dissertations, which serves several purposes. The first is that it represents proof that the dissertation was completed by the student and signed by the committee. Second, it facilitates submission to electronic dissertation databases, and third, it makes binding and placement into the university library's collection possible. One problem with submitting a dissertation has to do with its format. There is no guarantee that a university will accept a dissertation in the standard that was used, for example, to cite and reference other research. Some universities even require compliance with a standard, but then provide examples that don't match it, creating a question of which format to follow. Other universities require doctoral students to use complex typesetting and layout standards when submitting a dissertation, some of which are difficult or impossible to implement in most word processing applications. The problem here is not so much complying with a standard, but being able to do so timely so that a graduation window is not missed or costs do not pile up as a student goes through iterations of submission and rejection for failure to format the dissertation properly.

Jordyn ran into a problem complying with her university's dissertation format standards:

> I knew that the university required special standards when submitting a dissertation to the graduate school for binding, which of course were non-negotiable, but I had no idea that those standards were nearly impossible to reproduce in a word processing program, or that the university didn't warn students of the difficulties they might encounter trying to do so. For example, I had to format the dissertation like a book, which meant page numbers on the first page of a chapter had to be centered at the bottom of the page, and all subsequent page numbers in the chapter had to appear on outside edges of the pages at the top. This meant having to create many section breaks in the file, and that automatically changed where the tables, figures, and text appeared in the document. It took me two weeks to get it done, and I almost had to register for another semester since time was short for me to submit the dissertation.

Melanie also experienced trouble complying with her university's dissertation standards:

> The writing rubric I used to write my dissertation allowed present tense verbs when citing extant literature (e.g., "Smith argues that…"), but the university required the past tense (e.g., "Smith argued that…"), so I had to go through the entire dissertation and make the change. I was allowed to submit the dissertation two times before I incurred a cost for subsequent inspections. Each time I submitted the dissertation, there were always a few issues that needed to be fixed. Since the cost of subsequent submissions was progressive, I owed the thesis office hundreds of dollars in inspection fees. I found the process both unnecessary and unfair, but I had no choice in the matter.

Complying with a university's submission standards can be costly in both time and money. Before submitting your dissertation to the university, be sure you know all of the formatting standards with which you must comply. Also, consider using a standard for your dissertation that is the same as or that closely matches what the final dissertation will have to use. This way you minimize the changes you will have to make later. If it is obvious that you will have too much trouble doing any conversions yourself, hire a professional.

93
A Different World

Dissertations and journal articles share the common purpose of contributing to a field's literature, but whereas a journal article's only purpose is a contribution, dissertations have other purposes, such as being instruments of learning and adjudication. This means that there are practices associated with dissertations that are not part of journal articles. Dissertations are not simply journal articles that are lengthened by prolixity; they are a special form of research, and not knowing the difference means that recent graduates are sometimes confused by what should and shouldn't be included when creating articles from a dissertation.

The proposal usually comprises the bulk of a dissertation, but proposals initially serve as a means to judge whether a student and the study itself are ready to proceed. So, the proposal serves two purposes—first as a document of proof and then as the opening chapters of the dissertation. This dual purpose means that a proposal contains more than just the typical components found in the introduction, literature review, and methods sections of a journal article. It is common for proposals to include formal declarations of definitions, the researcher's position in the study, research questions, and paradigms under which the dissertation's topic is being examined. Some universities and committees require even more information, again as a means to judge both student and study. Once these components serve their purpose, they are not removed from the dissertation as extraneous information. This makes some students perceive that they are common to all forms of reporting research, even in journal articles. So, when recent graduates begin constructing journal articles from their dissertations, they include such information to create what they believe is a complete reporting of a study. Rhonda tried to include a little of everything from her dissertation when creating a journal article from it:

My dissertation was my only experience with conducting an empirical study, and so I used that experience when publishing my first journal article using data from my dissertation. I followed the structure of my dissertation by including, among other things, definitions of the terms that I used in the paper like I did in my dissertation. When I received the comments from the journal's editor and reviewers, they mentioned that I should remove the definitions because although it makes sense to define a term if used unconventionally in the paper, there is no need to define common terms or jargon that readers would already know. If I did need to define a term, I should do it in-text and give a citation if one is available; there was no need to include a separate definition section in the paper's introduction. It makes sense to me now, especially since I never saw a separate definition section in any journal article I have ever read.

Haruto included components from his dissertation in his first conference paper:

At the suggestion of my former chair, I submitted a version of my dissertation to a conference. The paper was accepted for presentation, but I was told that if I wanted the paper to appear in the conference proceedings, I needed to shorten it. The proceedings editor recommended that I remove the research questions, since I was clear in other parts of the paper why the study had been conducted, and research questions in the form of interrogatives was not common practice in conference papers. He mentioned that such information was redundant, and typically included only in a dissertation. I am glad that the proceedings editor was willing to be so helpful.

Since dissertations serve multiple purposes, some information common to them are not typically part of journal articles and other scholarly papers. Before submitting a dissertation as a journal or conference paper, look carefully at articles similar to the one being submitted to learn what parts pertain only to dissertations and therefore should not be included in the paper. The same is true of tables and figures, some of which are appropriate only in a dissertation. Recent graduates also commonly include unnecessary and lengthy appendices that served a purpose in the dissertation but are unlikely to be published in a journal, where pages are at a premium.

94
Trimming the Fat

It is common for doctoral students to reuse the content of their dissertations to construct one or more publications from them, which are then submitted to journals. After submission, the papers must go through the normal peer-review process to determine whether they are worthy of publication. However, many doctoral students make the mistake of thinking that a dissertation can be carved up into papers that resemble journal submissions. They treat the task as a simple cut-and-paste job, forgetting that the dissertation's chapters and sections were constructed to tell a story that might not be easily summarized in a smaller paper.

The average quantitative dissertation has 40,000 words, and the average journal article in the social sciences is 8,000 words. That means that to create a single paper from the dissertation, 32,000 words, or 80%, of the original text must be removed to accommodate a journal's length requirement. That is a lot of text, and choosing what content goes and what stays is difficult because by losing so much content, the essence and message of the dissertation is easily lost. Assuming that two papers can be constructed from a dissertation, that should mean that only 24,000 words, or 60%, of the dissertation must be removed. However, constructing papers from a larger work such as a dissertation does not work linearly. Even if two papers are constructed, they would share much of the same content, including the purposes of the studies, the designs, the methods, the samples, and even the analyses. Sometimes the only parts of such papers that are different are the variables analyzed, and associated findings. Students should try to get the best paper or papers that they can construct from their dissertation's content, but it is not as easy as selecting text to remove and sending what remains to a journal. Kenneth experienced trouble trying to construct a paper from his dissertation:

After I completed and defended my dissertation, my chair recommended that I begin publishing parts of my dissertation while it was still fresh in my mind. I started to look for ways to reduce the dissertation to a journal-length paper. My dissertation was about average length, but I still needed to cut a significant amount to get a paper out of it. I tried to include a little bit of everything in the paper, but then it just read like a shallow overview of the topic. Most of the arguments I made to justify the hypotheses were inadequate, and the explanation of the methods barely described what I had done. I now see the luxury that students have when writing their dissertations. They have so much room to discuss a topic, and there is much less need for them to economize their words.

Dennis tried to construct multiple papers from his dissertation:

The model I tested in my dissertation could easily be broken up into three smaller models for three separate journal articles. I recognized this back when I was constructing the model, so I thought it would be easy to get three publications soon after my dissertation was over. However, the models were not entirely independent, which meant that several variables and the relationships between them were shared across at least two models, and sometimes all three. Methodologically this was not a problem, but since the same data and analyses were used to test the three models, the three papers looked identical. This was also true since the purpose of testing the three models was the same, and they contributed to the same topic in the literature. Before submitting the papers to journals, I spent a long time making sure that the contributions of the three papers were different.

Journal articles are not miniature versions of a dissertation, and students often mistakenly believe that paring a dissertation to journal article length is easy. Getting more than one publication out of a dissertation is common, but it is challenging because there is often great overlap among the papers, and self-plagiarizing can lead to a researcher getting a bad reputation. Before turning a dissertation into journal articles, consider carefully what the papers contribute to the literature. If it is too small or repetitive, reconsider whether it should be sent to a journal.

95
Effort Equals Impact

Dissertations take a long time to complete, not just because they are difficult, but because they are conducted by inexperienced researchers, and the dissertation is pulled in many directions by the chair, committee, university, and even the student. During a dissertation, time seems to flow at different rates; first the days seem to crawl by, and later it seems that there isn't enough time to get everything done. This causes students to misperceive how long tasks are taking to complete, and leads to other misperceptions concerning the effort it takes to complete them. Even the contribution a dissertation is making to the literature is secondary to getting the dissertation finished, defended, and signed, creating even more misperceptions.

The struggles that students endure to produce a dissertation are worth it in the end because they make career goals possible, especially since doctorates open doors that are otherwise closed to people who lack the credentials to hold certain positions and perform well in them. Struggling with a dissertation is universal across universities, fields, and topics, and even people who have never conducted a dissertation refer to them allegorically for arduous tasks. A misperception that is not specific to dissertations is that if something is difficult and takes a long time to do, it must be worth quite a bit. That misperception causes people to think that they are underpaid, underappreciated, and overperforming. In the context of a dissertation, it makes students and recent graduates misperceive that since the dissertation was difficult and took a long time to complete, it must be making a huge contribution to the literature. Recent graduates are therefore disappointed and confused when they fail to publish their dissertations in a journal, or must make major changes to a paper because the editor and reviewers at a journal require them before the paper can be reconsidered for publication. The lesson here is that effort does not equal impact when it comes to dissertations. Karl learned this lesson when he submitted his dissertation to a journal:

> I graduated from a top university whose professors publish regularly in top journals in their fields. Having graduated from such a university, I was ready to place my name among those who publish in top journals. I submitted my dissertation to such a journal, but I was surprised when the paper was desk rejected, which means that the editor did not believe the paper could be published in the journal and so didn't send it out for review. He briefly mentioned that the methods I used did not coincide with the journal's standards because they were incapable of distinguishing substantive effects from method effects. I received similar comments from two other journals, and I had to settle for a middle journal in my field. I understand the editor's and the journal's position, but I wish I had realized it back when I was still working on my dissertation.

Jeanne misperceived the impact her dissertation would have on the literature:

> My dissertation was longer than average because I calculated many statistics to triangulate the findings. While working on the dissertation, I was motivated by the assumption that a lengthy dissertation meant that at least several papers could be published from it once I graduated. However, one of my colleagues mentioned that this was not true in my case because I couldn't publish more than one paper using the same data and variables just because each paper used different analyses. I talked it over with a few other colleagues, and they all independently agreed. So, I ended up with just one paper from my dissertation, and a harsh lesson in research.

Just because something is difficult and takes a long time to do does not mean it will have a huge impact. Dissertations serve several functions during a student's doctoral program, and that means that they include components not found in journal articles. The length of a dissertation is deceptive in that it appears that there is a lot of content that will serve a recent graduate well when it comes to publishing articles from it. However, overlap and the misperception that effort equals impact means that recent graduates are often left with less than what they think they have.

96
What Do You Think?

Chairs and committee members guide students through a dissertation, which makes students free to make mistakes knowing that there are people who will not allow the dissertation to degenerate into something that is unacceptable, even if those people provide no other advice than rejection of ideas. Students commonly dislike chairs and committees occasionally during a dissertation, but then miss them once the dissertation is over and the recent graduate must produce research without such aid. Colleagues and co-authors help, but there is another resource overlooked by inexperienced researchers when it comes to getting advice on research.

Publishing research as an independent researcher is not without its safety nets, though they are not as comprehensive as a chair and committee during a dissertation. University resources, colleagues, authors, and even the entire publishing process, with peer reviews and editorial evaluations, act as gatekeepers regarding whether research is worthy of publication, and where. Most of these resources are not guaranteed to produce objective advice; politics, unwillingness to speak badly about a colleague's research, and even apathy get in the way of honest appraisals. However, there is an alternative that is one of the most objective sources of research advice. Conferences are places where researchers can present their research ideas and findings, and get advice on how to improve them. Recalling what it was like to defend their dissertations, some recent graduates are reluctant to present at conferences, but during such presentations, the focus is not on judging the researcher or the research; it is about improving it. Opportunities to network and see what other researchers are working on make conferences a great place to improve both current and future research. Tracy was glad that she presented her research at a conference:

Before I published some of my dissertation's findings in a journal, I presented the paper at a national conference. The feedback I got from the conference reviews improved the paper, but the advice I received from those who attended my presentation was invaluable. I found that the advice people give at a conference is more real-world than the advice my chair and committee gave me during my dissertation. At the conference, the focus was on publishing the paper and its contribution, not on conforming to standards, meeting deadlines, and tweaking the study continuously. I used much of the advice I received, and although that meant revising the paper in several places, I believe that it also meant fewer changes once I received feedback from the journal. I also got a chance to attend other researchers' presentations, which gave me some ideas on the next studies I would conduct.

Lena benefitted from presenting at a conference in another way:

Research in my field is difficult because most of the data used are acquired from secondary sources, and there are only so many ways that the same data can be used repeatedly, even though the datasets contain millions of records. That means that publishing is difficult because proxies are scrutinized greatly. At the suggestion of my former chair, I took my dissertation to a conference to get some feedback and see how the people who contribute to the literature would view my approach to the data. I got some great feedback on how to improve my paper, and I also was able to start filling in my CV with activities that showed I was active with research. Attending conferences is almost required in my field, so having conference presentations on my CV shows that I am a serious researcher.

Conferences offer frank appraisals of research, and reflect an active research agenda. They do have some disadvantages. For example, it might take months for feedback from conference reviewers, which might hold up publication of a paper, and papers not selected for presentation means that the only feedback a researcher gets is the comments from the reviewers. However, when a paper is selected for presentation, a researcher receives much advice on how to improve a paper, and knows that the advice is objective since most of it comes from strangers. Conferences allow researchers at all levels to get honest feedback on a paper before submitting it to a journal, where desk rejection might derail its publication.

97
Ignoring the Experts

The chair is the most important person to a doctoral student during a dissertation, and since chairs have so much control over what a student does and does not do with a dissertation, it is natural for a student to think of a chair as a guru, a gatekeeper, and someone to admire and impress. However, like all researchers, chairs are limited to their own research experiences, and it is common for experienced researchers to be entrenched in paradigms, methods, and approaches to research that have made them successful. This makes chairs fallible, and some advice from them can be flawed.

Moving a career that involves scientific research forward is slow and tedious, and it requires a nascent researcher to be open to developments in the literature that will become trends in the near future. Identifying which developments will become the next big thing is essential to conducting cutting-edge research that contributes greatly to the literature. Relying on one source of information and advice on how to proceed as a researcher is tantamount to restricting yourself to one viewpoint. Drawing on expertise from multiple researchers offers the best chances of identifying the most important trends in the literature. During a dissertation, chairs are concerned with more than just a dissertation's contribution; they must also consider whether students are learning, and whether they are transitioning to researchers. Therefore, the advice they give and the tasks that they make students complete often consider more than just a single goal. Advice given during a dissertation might not apply outside of the dissertation, and therefore drawing from multiple experts to identify the next career direction is crucial. Walter realized that his chair's advice was not optimal to his career:

> Throughout my dissertation, my chair said that I should concentrate my study on publishing in a certain journal in which he publishes frequently.

The idea was that by concentrating on publication in the journal, conducting the study would seem more real and not just an exercise for getting through the program. After I graduated, I would have a dissertation that could be published in the journal more easily, getting me off to a good start with publishing research. However, when I casually discussed the matter with another researcher, she showed me that the focus of that journal did not fit the scope of the career I was aspiring to achieve; other journals would fit with my research and publishing goals much better. I am glad that I spoke with that other researcher because until I did, it never occurred to me that I wouldn't publish my dissertation in the journal my chair recommended.

Helen was also glad that she talked to another researcher:

Throughout both my program and dissertation, I was taught a method of conceptualizing and analyzing data that had several competitors in the literature. The reason the program concentrated so heavily on the method was that my chair and several other professors in the department were proponents of it, and they used it extensively in their own research. It makes sense that they would teach me what they know, but none of the alternatives were even mentioned during the program. Before I published my dissertation, I discussed it with a professor I got to know well during the dissertation, and he recommended that I consider using one of the other methods because it fit my data and purpose better. I haven't decided what I will do, but I am glad that he reminded me to consider other methods, not just the ones I was taught and am familiar with.

Chairs are doctoral students' most valuable resources during a dissertation. However, they represent only one source of information, and once a student graduates, it is time to start acting independently and decide what path will lead to the career the researcher wants. Talking with other researchers about career goals is the best way to identify alternatives and open the mind to possibilities that would otherwise have remained hidden. Researchers at all levels of ability and success use this technique frequently, so it makes sense to start using it from the beginning when a researcher has the most options from which to choose.

98
I Can Do It Myself

Dissertations and the students who produce them are guided by a chair and committee members because research is not something that can be conducted without experience. Lacking experience, students need people to judge, guide, and observe them so that the transition to researcher is possible. However, even after completing a doctoral program, recent graduates doubt their ability to conduct research, and for good reason. No one becomes an expert at something having done it only once. A dissertation typically represents the only study a recent graduate has ever conducted, so guidance even after graduation is a wise career move.

Publishing a dissertation is commonly the first thing recent graduates do after graduation. Recent graduates did not conduct their dissertations on their own; very knowledgeable and capable researchers guided them. Consequently, publishing a dissertation is not too difficult. What comes next can be frightening to recent graduates because they are now on their own to conduct new studies. At that point, nascent researchers suddenly realize how much their chairs and committee members contributed to their dissertations, and how comforting it was knowing that the committee acted as a kind of safety net that would not allow a student to self-destruct during the dissertation. Some recent graduates look to postdoctoral opportunities to hone their research skills and start networking with other researchers, but for others, such opportunities are not an option. One option to consider is partnering with experienced researchers to push a career forward, begin networking, and gain experience conducting research beyond a dissertation. Conducting research with experienced researchers is kind of like operating halfway between a dissertation and conducting research alone; you gain experience conducting original research, but do so under the watchful eye of someone who also has a stake in producing successful research. Sue discovered that finding a co-author was easier than expected:

> After I graduated, I presented part of my dissertation at a regional conference, and I began networking with other researchers in my field. I got to meet one of the researchers whose study I cited in my dissertation, and that made for a great icebreaker because before I knew it, we were discussing my dissertation's findings and the research that should follow. I asked her if she would be interested in conducting a study with me, and I was surprised when she said yes. We have already published the first study, and we are planning the next one now. I am glad that I not only attended that conference but was bold enough to ask an established researcher to conduct a study with me. She brought so many things to that first study, and I know that I never could have conducted such a study on my own.

Salvador also learned of the merits of conducting research with a co-author:

> Although I was very strong with methods, research design, and statistics during my dissertation, I was lacking in the ability to find gaps in the literature to fill. After I completed the dissertation, I knew that I needed to find some new research opportunities so that I could demonstrate my research ability to search committees looking to hire professors. I discussed the issue with one of my committee members, and he mentioned a study he was working on that I could join if I wanted to. I jumped at the chance, and he showed me a few ways he finds topics to study. Our relationship was more like a mentorship than a research partnership, but I have learned much about research since we have been working together, and I have met several other potential co-authors for future research.

Researchers at all stages of development partner with co-authors to take advantage of several benefits. The most important to a new researcher are making up for a lack of research skills, and developing those skills under the guidance of a more experienced researcher. Experienced researchers usually have an extensive network of co-authors from which to draw when looking for research partners, and even if they are not interested in conducting research with you, they might know someone who is. Don't struggle alone when there are many potential co-authors out there who are willing to conduct research with you.

99
Once Is Not Enough

Although dissertations represent real research in that they are conducted for and presented to a real audience, and they contribute to the literature like a journal article does, they also represent a special type of research, one whose purpose extends beyond just a contribution. Competing demands on a dissertation's purpose therefore disfigure it to include components that are not part of other types of research, and to exclude components of the same. Dissertations are also guided by a committee that keeps the study and the researcher on track. These elements make a dissertation a poor representation of the research process.

Researchers are independent thinkers who create knowledge on their own, and who are able and expected to operate without a chair, committee, department, dean, or university looking over their shoulders to ensure that the research they produce is both high-quality and contributory. The peer-review process is the gatekeeper that keeps flawed research from contaminating the literature, whereas that function is carried out by individuals during a dissertation. These characteristic disparities between research conducted as a dissertation and research conducted outside of a dissertation demonstrate that transitioning from one to the other is fraught with pitfalls that can take recent graduates by surprise. Although getting advice from colleagues by, for example, presenting at a conference is available, such advice can be acquired only after an entire study is complete and at least a rough draft of a paper is written. Apprehension about looking foolish in front of colleagues and more experienced researchers causes some recent graduates to perceive that they are all alone when developing research. This makes them vulnerable to procrastination with their research programs, and they sometimes fall so far behind there is no way to rectify the problem. Amahle experienced difficulties getting a research program off the ground:

I landed a tenure-track professorship at a university soon after I graduated, and after I published my dissertation, I moved on to developing a new research program, but I had difficulty identifying gaps in the literature to fill. During my dissertation, I thought that my chair did not provide much guidance, and that she could have done more to help me finish my program quicker and with fewer roadblocks. Now that I had no one to go to for help whenever I needed it, I found myself unsure of whether I could even produce any research at all, let alone any that would count toward getting tenure. I tried to get help from colleagues, but I didn't want to bother them and they always seemed too busy to help. It took me a long time to get on track with my research and start producing something that made sense.

Seth also had trouble getting started with his research:

My first job in a university was hectic. One minute I was a struggling doctoral candidate, and the next I was a struggling professor. I thought that my dissertation was extraordinarily difficult, but at least at the time that's all I had to concentrate on. As a professor, I had university training to complete, classes to teach, papers to grade, and engagement with the community to work on. I was pulled in multiple directions, and the one thing that was unstructured—my research—suffered. It was difficult finding time to work on research, and I always had somewhere else to put my time. Unlike the dissertation, there were no clear deadlines or milestones, and I ended up conducting no research my first year as a professor. It made life difficult because I knew I was behind, but I didn't know where to find the time to get it done.

Tasks expand to fill the time available to do them, and without someone to prod a researcher to work on a study, it is easy to fill time with other tasks. Researchers are like entrepreneurs; they must be self-starters, take risks, set their own milestones, and be satisfied with what they've accomplished, even when no one congratulates them on their successes. Researchers who lack these traits let time slip by until they reach a point of no return, at which some very difficult decisions must be made regarding their motivation, their research, and their jobs.

100
If You Love It, Let It Go

Doctoral students have a love–hate relationship with their dissertations, which depends on when you ask students how they feel about them. Students hate dissertations while conducting them because they are arduous, are tedious, and never seem to end. However, after graduation, former students have trouble letting go of their dissertations. They have so much invested in them that they want to get as much out of them as they can. Coupled with a few other issues that pop up in their first jobs, recent graduates milk a dissertation for all its worth, leading to even more problems with research and careers.

It is natural to feel pride after completing a dissertation, primarily because it accompanies graduation, means freedom from the doctoral program, and signals the beginning of a career. So much time and effort goes into a dissertation that it is also natural for recent graduates to want it to do as much for them as possible. Some recent graduates are also concerned about conducting research on their own, and they hide behind their dissertations, convincing themselves that more can be pulled from them so that they can avoid starting new research programs. This type of thinking leads to several negative consequences that can hurt a career in the future, especially when it comes to tenure and promotions. However, the delayed effect makes recent graduates unaware of those consequences. Vital to understanding a dissertation's role in a career is knowing when to put it on the shelf and move on to other studies, but with so many motivators keeping the dissertation off the shelf, it is difficult to do. The dissertation is real and tangible, and future research is only an idea, making it seem that the former is a greater asset than the latter. Alma had trouble letting go of her dissertation:

My dissertation used a large sample, which meant that papers I published from it had great statistical power. Collecting so much data again was unappealing to me, so I kept publishing papers using my dissertation's data. After the third paper was published, my department held its annual review of tenure-track professors and assessed our research. One member of the evaluation committee looked carefully at my publications and noticed that the n-size of each was the same. She asked about it and I told her that I had used the same dataset for each, and that I had two more studies planned for the data. The committee voiced concerns with that approach because it went against the university's research principles. I had to stop using the dataset and move on to new studies.

Enrique also used his dissertation's dataset extensively:

During my dissertation, I collected variables from participants, such as age, salary, education, etc., that never made it into the study. They were originally going to be control variables, but my committee had me change my model so they never got used. I published my dissertation's model, and then started creating new models by adding those unused variables one at a time to the original model, evaluating how it changed the relationships in the model. I published these models in several journals, so I was unaware that there was a problem with publishing multiple studies from the same data, and adding only one variable to the same model at a time. The head of the tenure committee mentioned that I was conducting very incremental research, and it would not look good when it came time for the final tenure evaluation. I'm glad I found out before it was too late.

The dissertation is the center of a doctoral candidate's life, and there is nothing better than holding a bound edition of a completed dissertation in hand, knowing that it is over and never has to be done again. However, a dissertation can also be addicting, and recent graduates sometimes use a dissertation as a crutch and excuse not to conduct new research. At some point, especially after a study is published from it, the dissertation should be abandoned so that a career can advance. Too much reliance on a dissertation is unhealthy to a career, and like a bad habit, it needs to be dropped so better opportunities can be pursued.

SUGGESTIONS WELCOME

This book reflects input from many people, especially the students who candidly shared their experiences and allowed me to use them to help other doctoral students avoid the most common mistakes made during dissertations. I am indebted to them for the contributions they made to this book's approach. I encourage readers to contribute to future editions of this book by sharing their thoughts on the current edition. Send praise, criticisms, suggestions, anecdotes, and other comments to:

Suggestions@ScienceSurvivalAcademy.com

I thank all who contribute to subsequent editions, and I wish all who read this book the best of luck with their dissertations.

www.ingramcontent.com/pod-product-compliance
Lightning Source LLC
Chambersburg PA
CBHW070033100426
42740CB00013B/2677